# LogoWare

*How new software is changing logo design*

Editor
**David E. Carter**

Book Designer
**Suzanna M.W. Brown**
Additional Graphics
**Christa Carter**

**LogoWare — The best 34 programs for creating digital logos.**

First published 1998 by Hearst Books International
1350 Avenue of the Americas
New York, NY 10019

ISBN: 0688-15348-8

Distributed in the U.S. and Canada by
Watson-Guptill Publications
1515 Broadway
New York, NY 10036
Tel: (800) 451-1741
(732) 363-4511 in NJ, AK, HI
Fax: (732) 363-0338

Distributed throughout the rest of the world by
Hearst Books International
1350 Avenue of the Americas
New York, NY 10019
Fax: (212) 261-6795

ISBN: 0-8230-6602-9



Printed in Hong Kong by Everbest Printing Company
through Four Colour Imports, Louisville, Kentucky.

# When I started this book,

I wrote to a large number of logo designers and asked them to send me some work for possible inclusion in this publication. I also asked that they let me know which software product had been used to create each design.

The results were no surprise. Adobe Photoshop, Adobe Illustrator, and Macromedia Freehand were the dominant choices.

The opening section of this book includes many outstanding designs which are created by designers using these three programs.

But as powerful as the "Big Three" creative programs are, I knew that there were some very good products out there that were highly effective in the logo creation process. I also felt that designers are looking for new visuals to make their work stand out from the pack.

So, I acquired and tested a large number of other programs. The bulk of this book includes examples of graphics which can be created by these other programs. In many cases, I did not create sample logos, but felt compelled to show specific graphic styles which these programs can produce. I think you'll be pleased by the way they are presented.

Finally, I included a large amount of clip art (See "Using Clip Art as a Logo" on page 144.)

This book on logo design software is the first of its kind. For everyone who wants to design unique, effective logos, this is your source to the very best software products available today.

-Dave

## Adobe Photoshop

**Adobe Photoshop 4.0** is the master manipulation tool when working with photographs on the computer.

Mask

Client
*Autograph Authority*
Design Firm
**Muller + Company**
Kansas City, Missouri

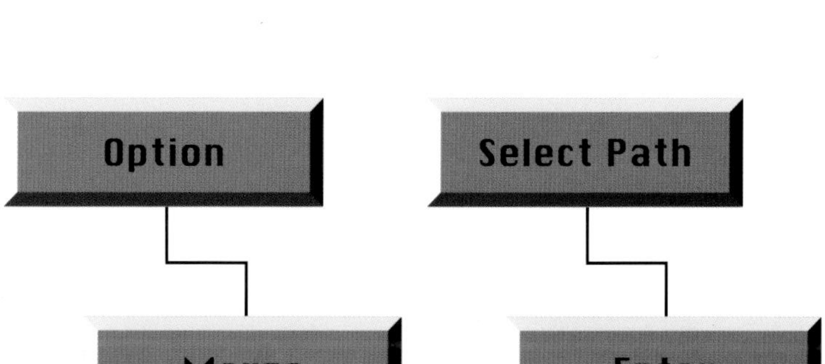


Client
*Wichita Public Schools/Wichita Area*
Design Firm
**Love Packaging Group**
Wichita, Kansas

Blitz Research, Inc.

3-D Filter

Client
*Blitz Research,Inc.*
Design Firm
**Image Associates, Inc.**
Raleigh, North Carolina

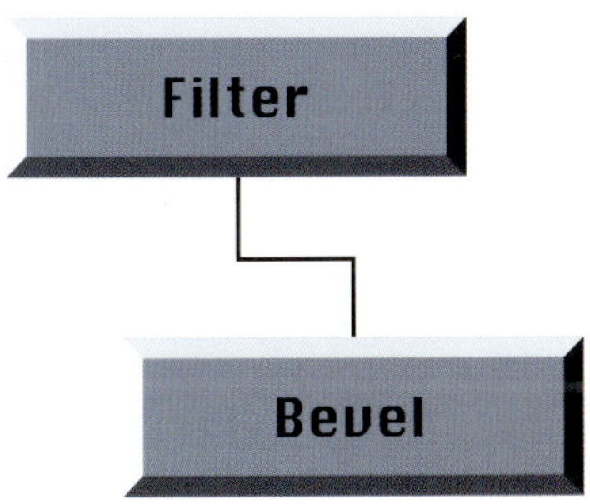


Client
*Care Touch*
Design Firm
**Image Associates, Inc.**
Raleigh, North Carolina

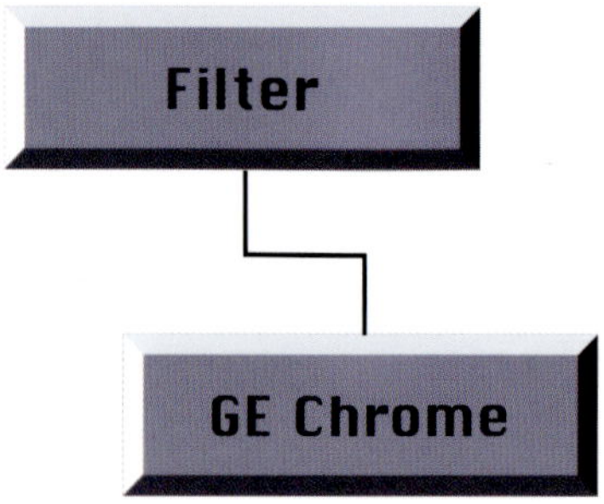


Client
*Certified Angus Beef*
Design Firm
**Love Packaging Group**
Wichita, Kansas

Client
*The Coffee Millers*
Design Firm
**Love Packaging Group**
Wichita, Kansas

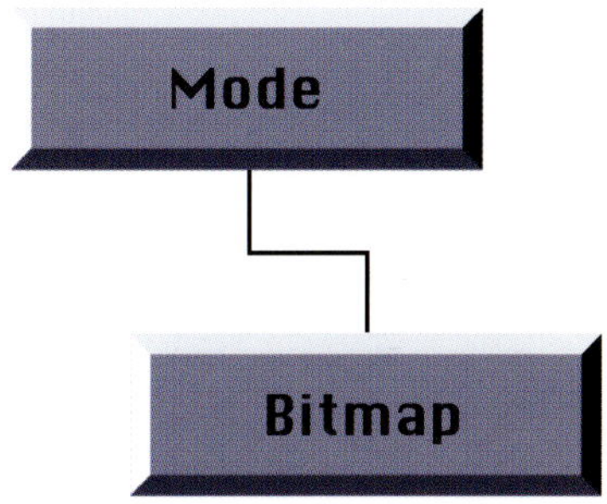


Client
*dreyfus + associates Photography*
Design Firm
**CUBE Advertising & Design**
St. Louis, Missouri

Client

*Intercourse with a Vampire*

Design Firm

**Mike Salisbury Communications**

Torrance, California

Design Firm
**Wet Paper Bag Graphic Design**
Fort Worth, Texas

Perspective

Shear

Transparency

Blur Tool

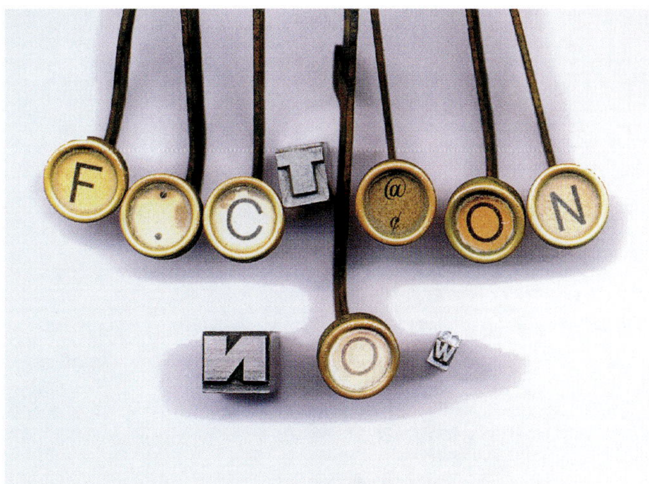

Client
*Fiction Now*
Design Firm
**Mike Salisbury Communications**
Torrance, California

Filter

KPT 3.0 Glass Lens

Client

*Elogen, Inc.*

Design Firm

**Love Packaging Group**

Wichita, Kansas

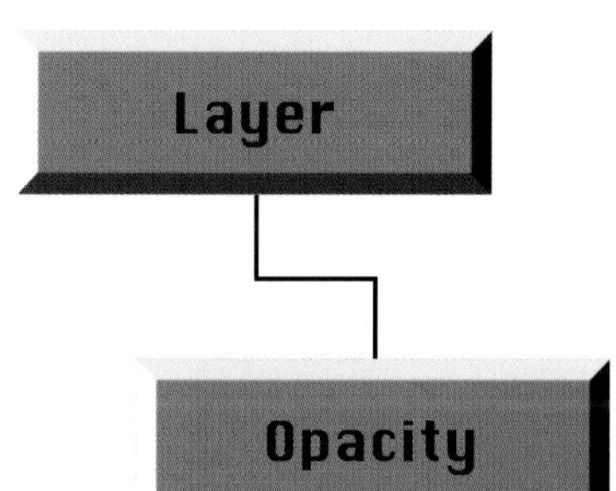


Client

*The Fantastic World of Gourmet Chocolate*

Design Firm

**Love Packaging Group**

Wichita, Kansas

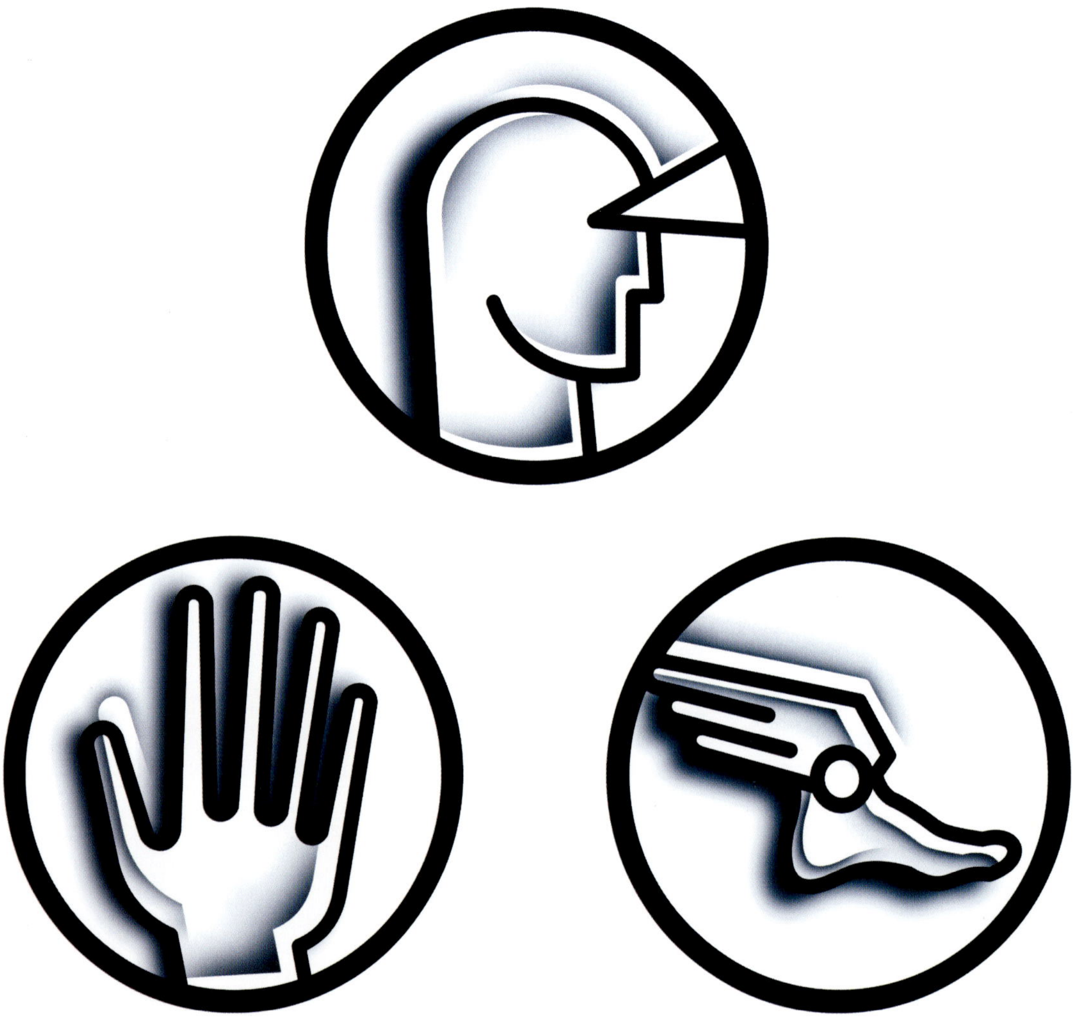

Paste as Paths

Airbrush

Client

*HOC Industries*

Design Firm

**Love Packaging Group**

Wichita, Kansas

INTEGRO™

Client

*Integro*

Design Firm

**Image Associates, Inc.**

Raleigh, North Carolina

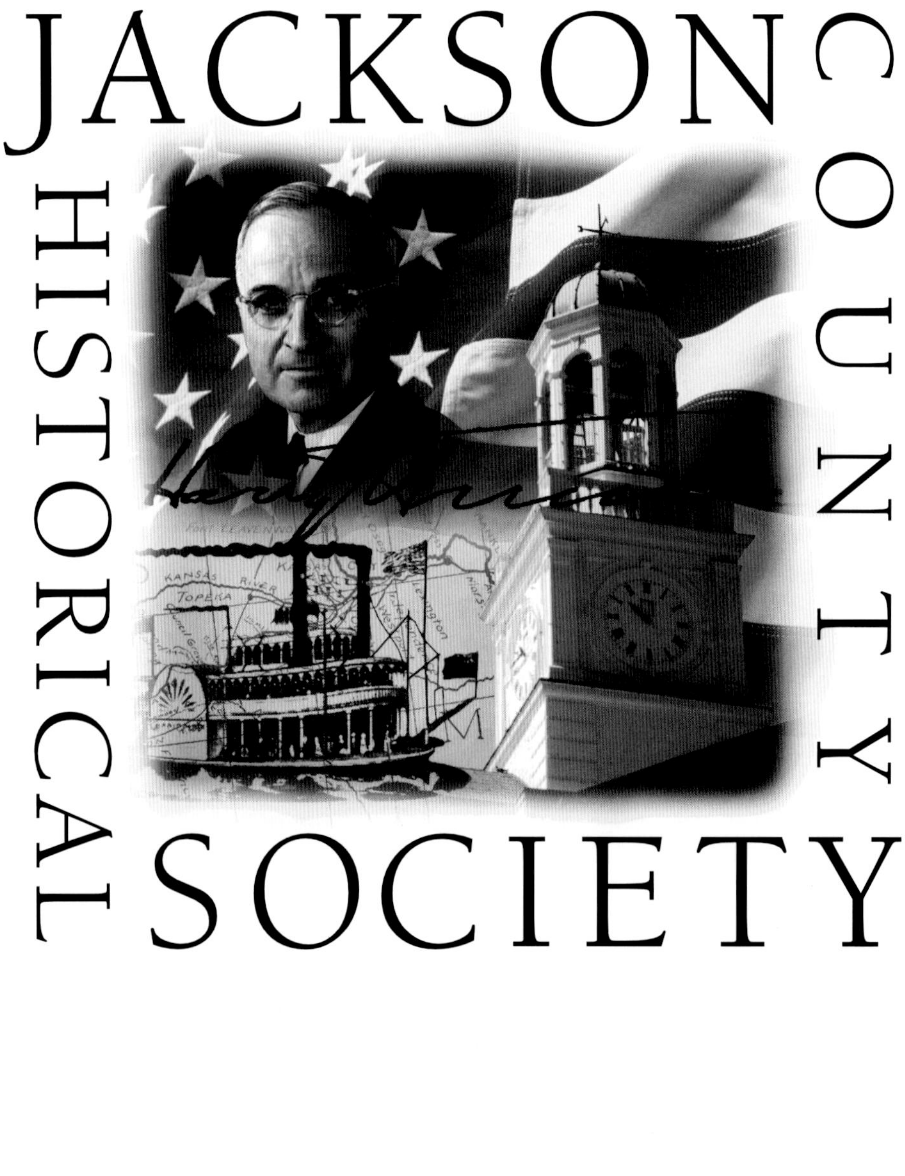


Layers

Client
*Jackson County Historical Society*
Design Firm
**Muller + Company**
Kansas City, Missouri

Client
*OmniMedia*
Design Firm
**After Hours Creative**
Phoenix, Arizona

Client
*MindJourney, LLC*
Design Firm
**Image Associates, Inc.**
Raleigh, North Carolina

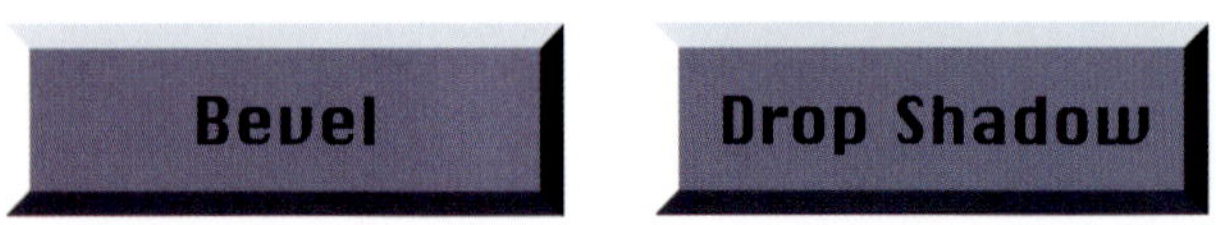


Client
*Unistar*
Design Firm
**Designation**
New York, New York

LogoWare

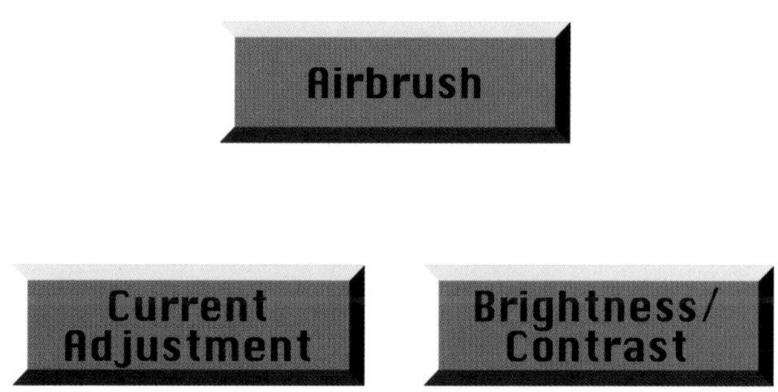


Client
*Mike Regnier*
Design Firm
**Muller + Company**
Kansas City, Missouri

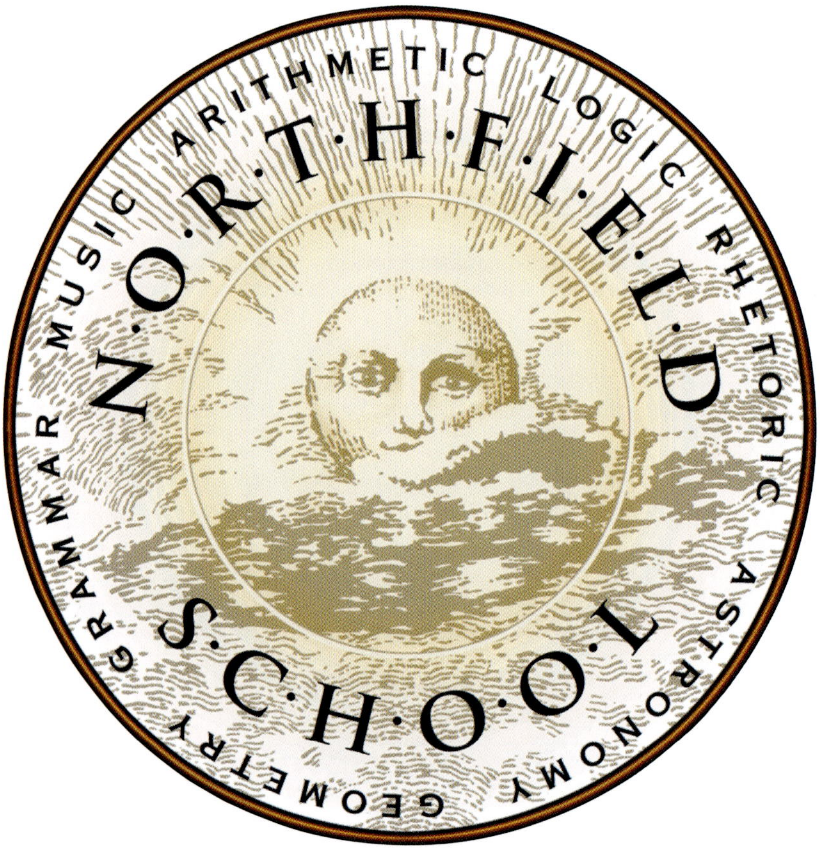


Layer

Opacity

Client

*Northfield School*

Design Firm

**Love Packaging Group**

Wichita, Kansas

Client

*Pardners Unlimited, Inc.*

Design Firm

**Love Packaging Group**

Wichita, Kansas

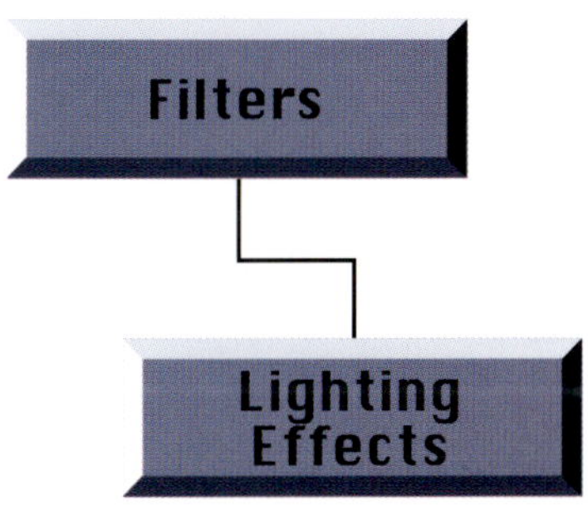

3-D Modeling

Client
*Seattle Square*
Design Firm
**Hansen Design Company**
Seattle, Washington

Client
*Toshiba*
Design Firm
**Designation**
New York, New York

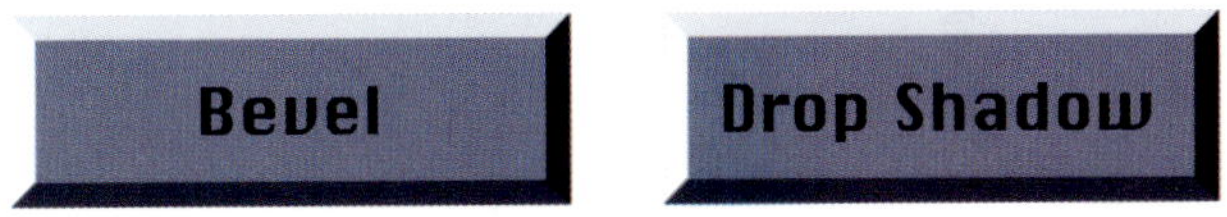

Client
*Culinary Arts and Entertainment*
Design Firm
**After Hours Creative**
Phoenix, Arizona

Client

*Saint Louis Zoo*

Design Firm

**CUBE Advertising & Design**

St. Louis, Missouri

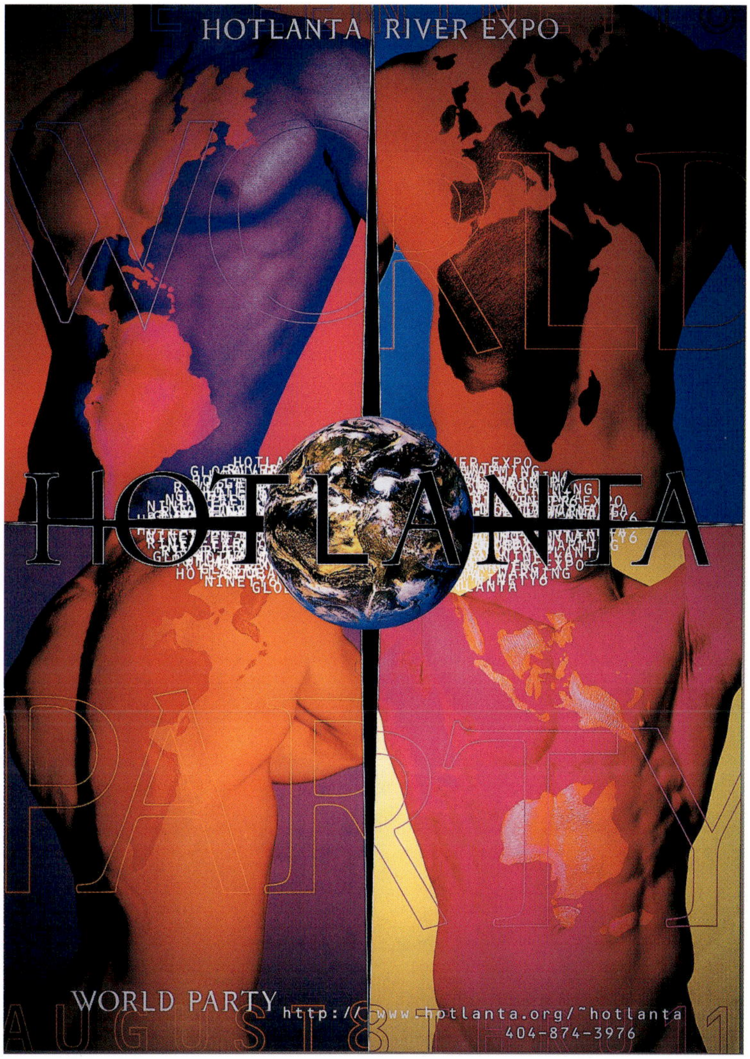


Client

*Hotlanta River Expo*

Design Firm

**After Hours Creative**

Phoenix, Arizona

While Adobe Photoshop is best known as a photo editing program, it has many filters which can be applied to basic line art to create some exciting visual techniques for logos. To show some of these filters, we started with the basic "globe" logo at right. Then, different filters were applied to the artwork. The results are shown on these two pages.

Original design

Crystal

Emboss

Ripple

Twirl

Pinch

Add Noise

Color Halftone

Difference Clouds

Fragment

Lens Flare

Lighting Effects

Mezzotint

Mosaic

Motion Blur

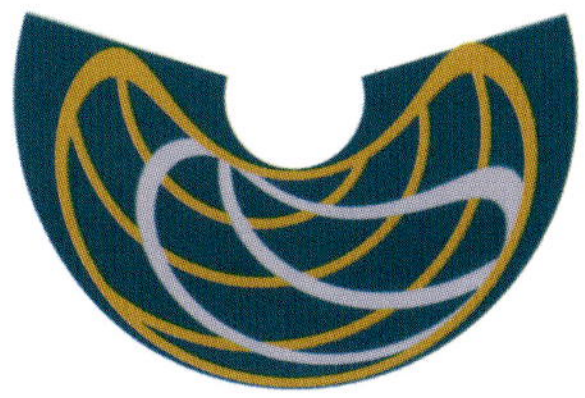

Polar Coordinates

Pointillize 4

Pointilllize 14

Radial Blur

Spherize

Wind Blast

Zig Zag

# Adobe Illustrator

Adobe Illustrator 6.0 is a multi-faceted drawing program that lends itself to page design as well.

Client
*Dix Productions*
Design Firm
**Muller + Company**
Kansas City, Missouri

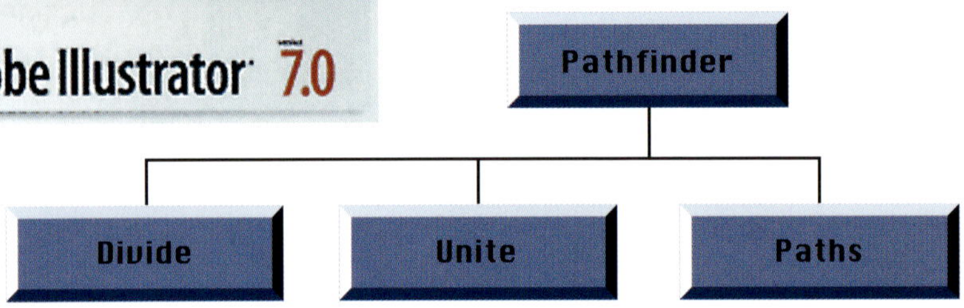


DIX PRODUCTIONS

---

Client
*Digital Archaeology*
Design Firm
**Muller + Company**
Kansas City, Missouri

DIGITAL ARCHAEOLOGY

Mask Gradient

---

Client
*The Stock Market*
Design Firm
**Designation**
New York, New York

Distort

DISC express™

Client
*Advantage Electronic Billing*
Design Firm
**Damion Hickman Design**
Newport Beach, California

All logos on this page use the same commands.

Filter

Outline Font

Unite

Client
*Damion Hickman Design*
Design Firm
**Damion Hickman Design**
Newport Beach, California

Client
*Master Development Corporation*
Design Firm
**Damion Hickman Design**
Newport Beach, California

Client

*Park Meadows Mall*

Design Firm

**Communication Arts Inc.**

Boulder, Colorado

This logo also utilized Adobe Streamline.

Roughen

Client

*Bagel Works Bread Company*

Design Firm

**Muller + Company**

Kansas City, Missouri

This logo also utilized Adobe Streamline.

Roughen

Client

*Texas Christian University (TCU)*
*Department of Journalism*

Design Firm

**Wet Paper Bag Graphic Design**

Fort Worth, Texas

Filter

Distort

Roughen

Client

*Colorado Brewery*

Design Firm

**Communication Arts Inc.**

Boulder, Colorado

Client
*Helen Woodward Animal Center*
Design Firm
**Tracy Sabin**
San Diego, California

Client
*UCSD*
Design Firm
**Tracy Sabin**
San Diego, California

Client
*Rubio's Baja Grill*
Design Firm
**Tracy Sabin**
San Diego, California

Client
*Magic Carpet Books*
Design Firm
**Tracy Sabin**
San Diego, California

Client
*Monkey Studios*
Design Firm
**Tracy Sabin**
San Diego, California

Client
*Rubio's Baja Grill*
Design Firm
**Tracy Sabin**
San Diego, California

Client
*Maddox Design*
Design Firm
**Tracy Sabin**
San Diego, California

Client
*The Phantom*
Design Firm
**Mike Salisbury Communications**
Marina Del Rey, California

Client
*Ed Wood*
Design Firm
**Mike Salisbury Communications**
Marina Del Rey, California

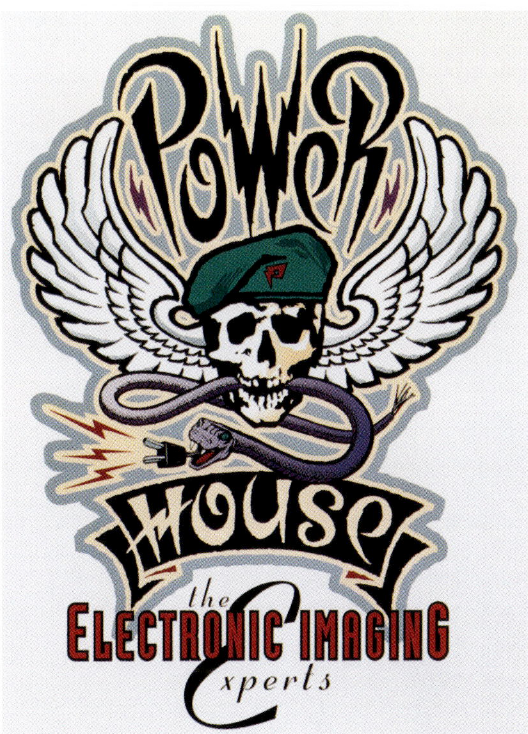


Client
*Power House*
Design Firm
**Mike Salisbury Communications**
Marina Del Rey, California

Client

*Explornet/North Carolina Netday*

Design Firm

**Image Associates, Inc.**

Raleigh, North Carolina

This logo also utilized Adobe Photoshop.

---

**Gaussian Blur**

Client

*Society of Comtemporary Photography*

Design Firm

**Muller + Company**

Kansas City, Missouri

This logo also utilized Adobe Photoshop.

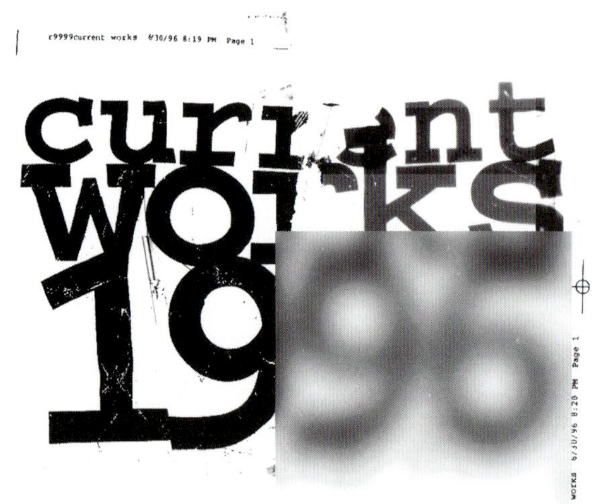


---

**Mask**

Client

*Fuch's*

Design Firm

**Muller + Company**

Kansas City, Missouri

This logo also utilized Adobe Photoshop.

Client

*DACOM*

Design Firm

**Alfonso Brothers**

Montreal, Canada

This logo also utilized Adobe Photoshop.

Client

*Superior*

Design Firm

**Muller + Company**

Kansas City, Missouri

This logo also utilized Adobe Photoshop.

Client

*Dead Man Walking*

Design Firm

**Mike Salisbury Communications**

Marina Del Rey, California

This logo also utilized Adobe Photoshop.

Client
*The Cape*
Design Firm
**Mike Salisbury Communications**
Marina Del Rey, California

---

Client
*Gotcha Cat*
Design Firm
**Mike Salisbury Communications**
Marina Del Rey, California

---

Client
*The Mask of Zorro*
Design Firm
**Mike Salisbury Communications**
Marina Del Rey, California

Pathfinder

Divide

Client
*Gambucci's*
Design Firm
**Muller + Company**
Kansas City, Missouri

Client
*Computer Sciences Corporation*
Design Firm
**Ramona Hutko Design**
Bethesda, Maryland

Reflect

Client
*Glass Tiger*
Design Firm
**Alfonso Brothers**
Montreal, Canada

Client
*Jennifer Sands the Talking Psychic*
Design Firm
**Tracy Sabin**
San Diego, California

---

Client
*Custom Cars*
Design Firm
**Tracy Sabin**
San Diego, California

---

Client
*Chaos Lures*
Design Firm
**Tracy Sabin**
San Diego, California

Client
*Goods for Guns Foundation*
Design Firm
**Designation Inc.**
New York, New York

Client
*Themeware, Inc.*
Design Firm
**Damion Hickman Design**
Newport Beach, California

This logo also utilized Fractal Design Painter.

Distort

Distort Clone

Client
*Napa Valley Gourmet Salsa Co.*
Design Firm
**Damion Hickman Design**
Newport Beach, California

Client

*Red Ant*

Design Firm

**Mike Salisbury Communications**

Marina Del Rey, California

---

Client

*Rage Magazine*

Design Firm

**Mike Salisbury Communications**

Marina Del Rey, California

---

Client

*Angels*

Design Firm

**Mike Salisbury Communications**

Marina Del Rey, California

Client

*Hot Rod Hell*

Design Firm

**Tracy Sabin**

San Diego, California

Client

*Stuffit*

Design Firm

**Mike Salisbury Communications**

Marina Del Rey, California

Client

*Odyssey*

*Harcourt Brace & Co.*

Design Firm

**Tracy Sabin**

San Diego, California

# Adobe Texturemaker

Adobe TextureMaker is a gallery of more than 100 templates of realistic textures. Categories include fabrics, geometrics, liquids, marbles, metals, and woods.

You may use any illustration to carve into a texture, and you have additional control with a series of slide bars. For the logo designer, this product can give you a distinctive foundation for a logo.

A variety of foundation textures are shown here.

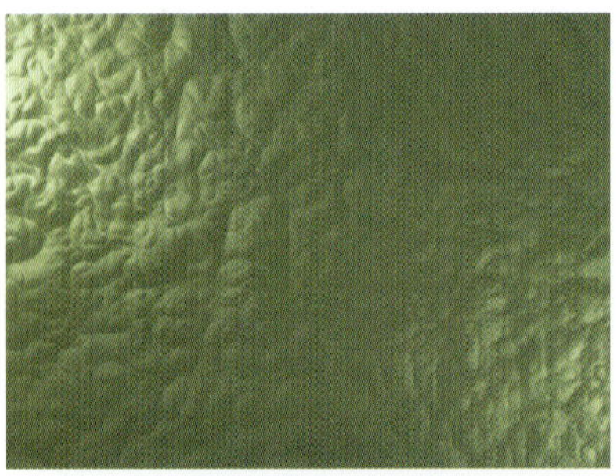

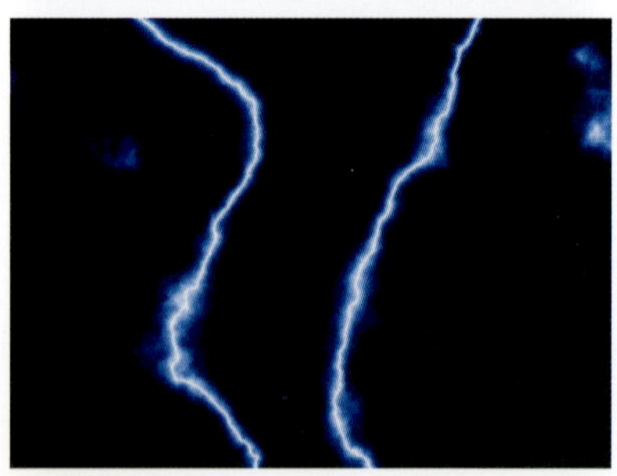

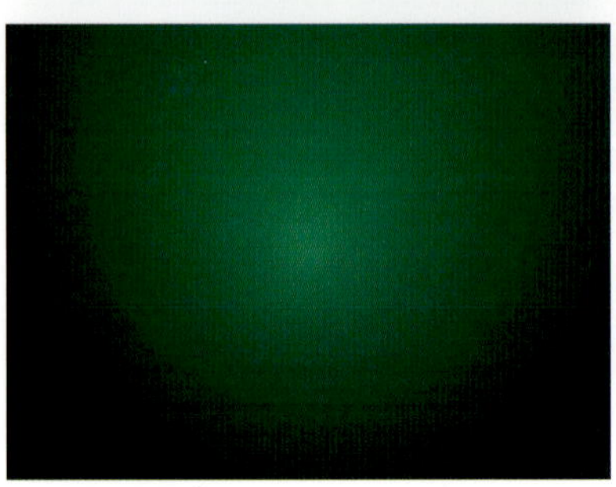

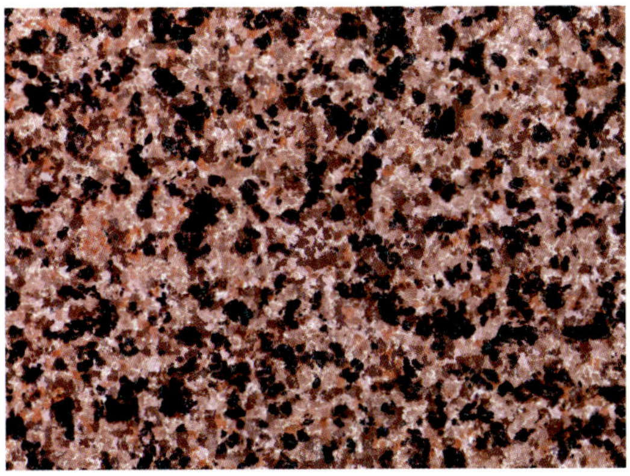

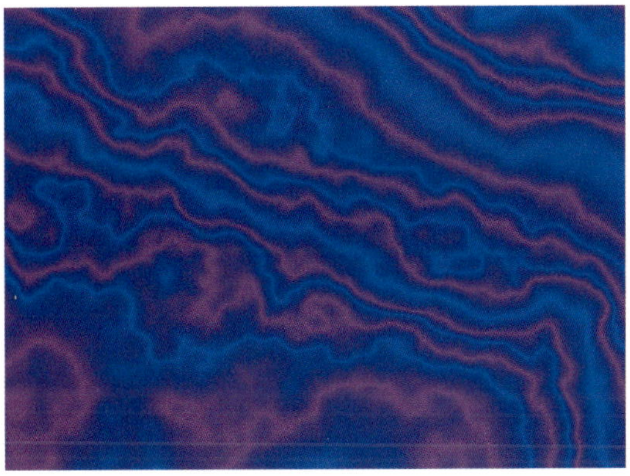

The logo at right was created by using one of the color backgrounds, then taking it into FreeHand. There a circle was drawn, the background was cut; then the background was "pasted inside" a circle (with invisible line).

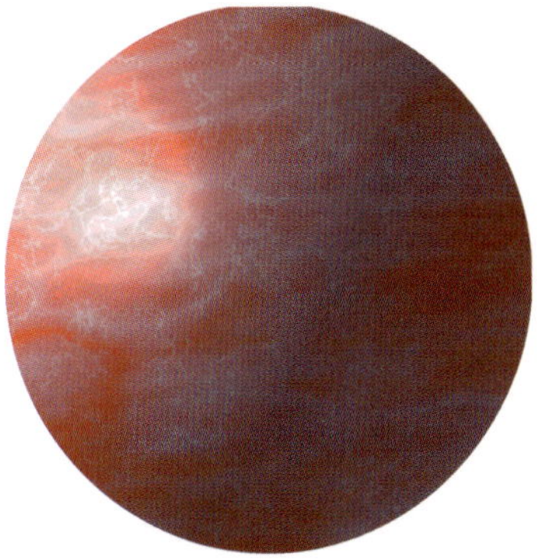

***The Red Planet***

Adobe TextureMaker is a product of Adobe Corporation, 1585 Charleston Road, P.O. Box 7900, Mountain View, CA 94039-7900.

# Adobe After Effects

Adobe After Effects is a high-end program for creating motion graphics on the desktop. The user can quickly produce on-air promos, commercials, music videos, and complex special effects and, yes, LOGOS. The ability to animate a logo is at your fingertips with this product, and best of all, these features can be used for print media, as you can export a single frame.

There is a great deal of power in the filters of After Effects since you can change the look of a graphic with the flick of the mouse. The "gears" shown on these pages begin as somewhat basic, but they show how this product can rapidly change the look—whether with animation or as a still.

While Adobe After Effects is primarily a motion graphics tool, it can also be used to create visuals for print media.

You can control complex on-screen animation frame-by-frame with Adobe After Effects.

Brush Strokes

Spherize

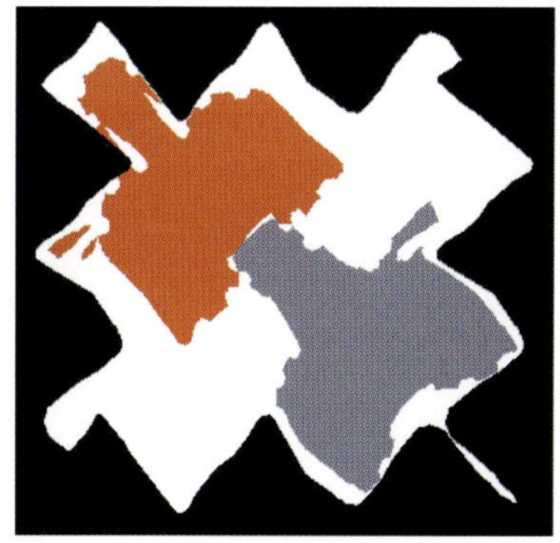

Wave

Polar Coordinates

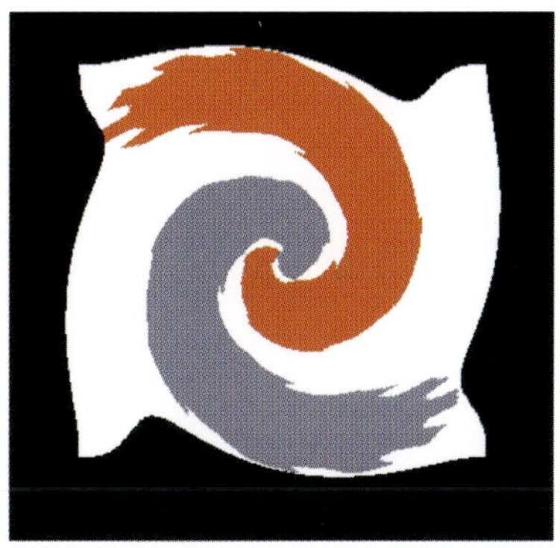

Twirl

Zig Zag

Lens Flare

Blur

Mosaic

Adobe After Effects is a product of Adobe Corporation, 1585 Charleston Road, P.O. Box 7900, Mountain View, CA 94039-7900.

# DigiEFFECTS: Aurorix, Berserk & Cyclonist

DigiEFFECTS has three great plug-ins for Adobe After Effects. In fact, Aurorix, Berserk, and Cyclonist are such exciting graphics products that I could see why someone would buy Adobe After Effects just to get a program that would allow the use of the plug-ins. And—they all can be done with a great deal of variation with various slider controls.

That said, I must say that all the effects are easy to use, and they include effects with titles such as: chaotic rainbow, noise blender, light zoom, earthquake, soap film, warpoid, bulgix, tilos, flitter, whirlix, video look, woodmaker, infinity warp, strange nebulae, laser, edgex, pearls, for bank, still noise, oil paint, spintron, squisher, and my personal favorite, starfield.

We started with a photo of Mona Lisa (one of the sample files in Adobe After Effects).

Color Spotlights

3D Lighting

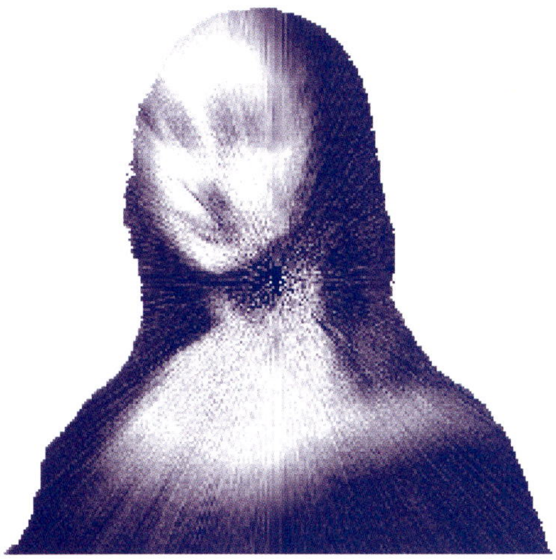

Light Zoom

Aged Film

Tilos

Using the DigiEFFECTS plug ins for Adobe After Effects, we started with an "Atomic" logo. By using the simple plug ins, all the designs shown were created in a matter of minutes.

Blizzard

3-D Lighting

Spintron

Cyclo Warp

Laser

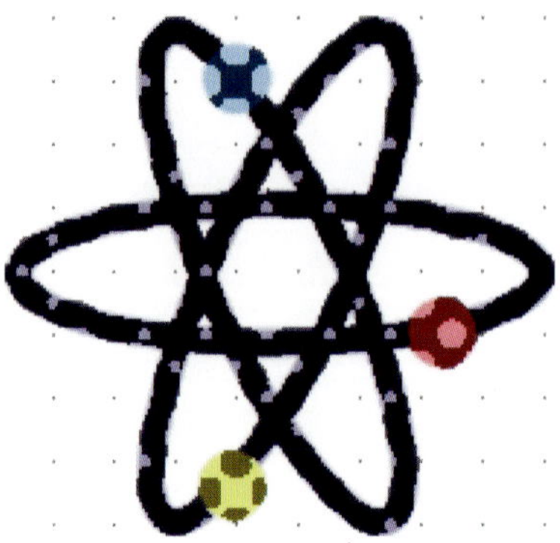

News Print

Star Field

Still Noise

Van Goughist

Video Look

Original

Contourist

Crystallizer

Cyclo Warp

Fog Bank

Oil Paint

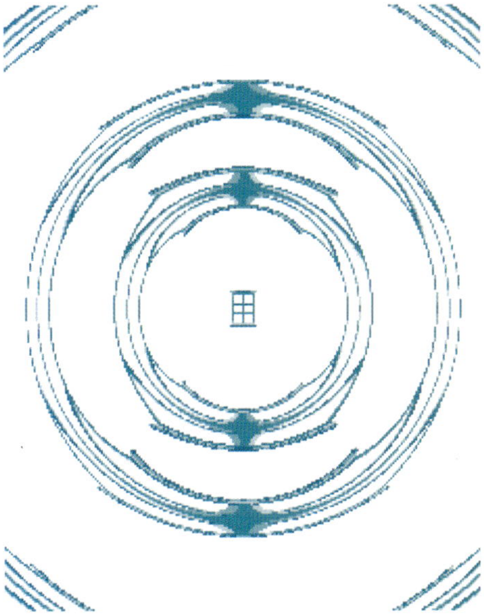

Ripploid

Van Goughist

DigiEFFECTS products are available from DigiEffects, 1817 California St., Suite 203, San Francisco, CA 94109. Phone: (415) 563-4318. Fax: (415) 563-3245. www.digieffects.com.

# Stylist

Stylist is an easy-to-use plug in for Adobe Illustrator 6.0 that lets you quickly modify lines, art, etc. The product includes a floating palette with a non-modal interface that makes style sheets constantly accessible. Even a novice user can select and apply styles to lines and type just by clicking on the various controls.

Fonts can be modified in many ways with this easy-to-use system, and various unusual treatments such as outlines, shadows, etc. are easily made with Stylist.

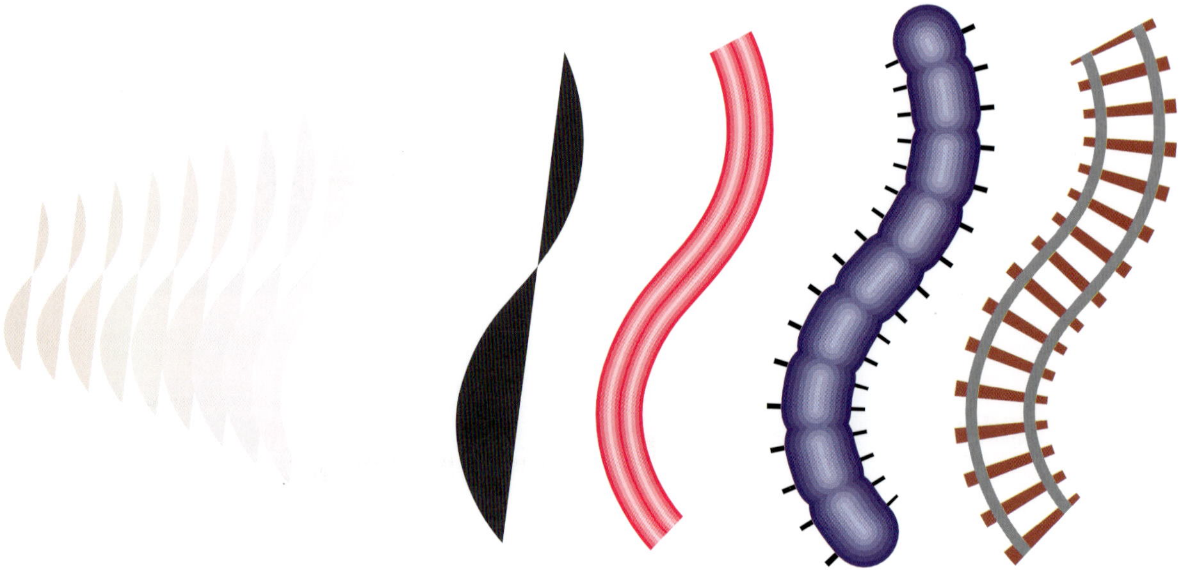

Vertigo 3D Dizzy is available from Vertigo Technology Inc., 1255 West Pender St., Vancouver, BC Canada V6E 2V1. Phone: (604) 684-2113. Fax: (604) 684-2108. www.vertigo3d.com.

# Eye Candy

Eye Candy 3.0 (formerly Black Box 2.0) is a series of Photoshop filters that have some exciting, quickly-executed special effects. Some of the categories are smoke, fire, chrome, weave, antimatter, carve, glass, jiggle, fur, and squint. Each module has controls which allow you to make modifications—while you see the change happen.

Author's note: *I had planned to allocate two pages for this product. However, one exciting Sunday afternoon, I began playing (that's the right word) with Eye Candy and came up with enough good material to fill much more space. These four pages give you a good overview of just what Eye Candy can do for you.*

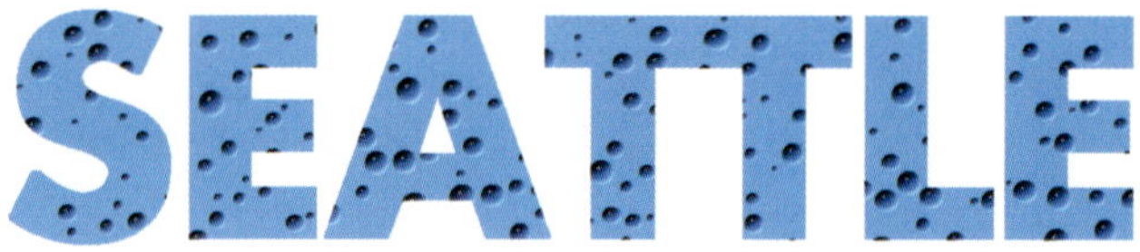


Water Drop

Fur—Typical

Glow

Chrome—Mercury

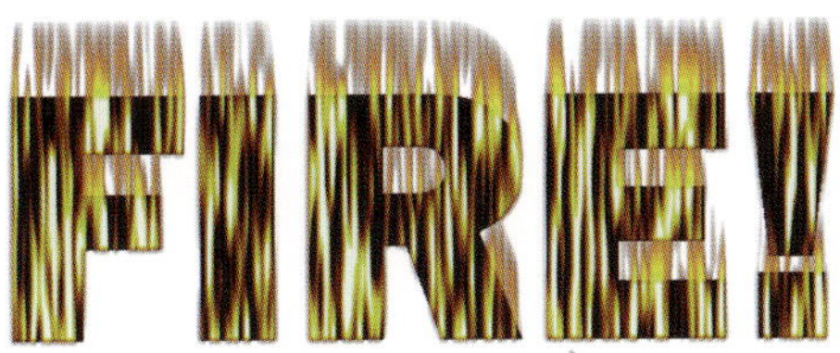


Fire—Burning Inside

Fire—Chrome-Like

Fire—Glowing Coal

Drop Shadow—Blue Eye Shadow

Drop Shadow—Stark

In the Photoshop section there is a two-page spread (26 - 27) showing a basic "globe" logo along with the various treatments that can be done using Photoshop Filters. Since Eye Candy is basically some specialized Photoshop plug-in filters, I started with the same basic globe logo, then applied some of the filters to demonstrate how they work with art.

Original Logo

Jiggle Twisty

Glass - Cola Bottle

Jiggle - Extreme Jitter

Water Drops

Smoke - Pollution

Motion Trail/
Moving Fast

Jiggle Twisty

Squint

Swirl - Little Crystals

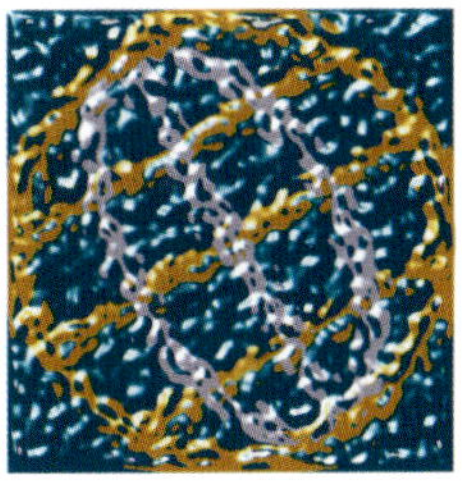

Glass - Iluminated Lumps

Flames - Glowing Coal

Weave

Original Logo, with Background Removed

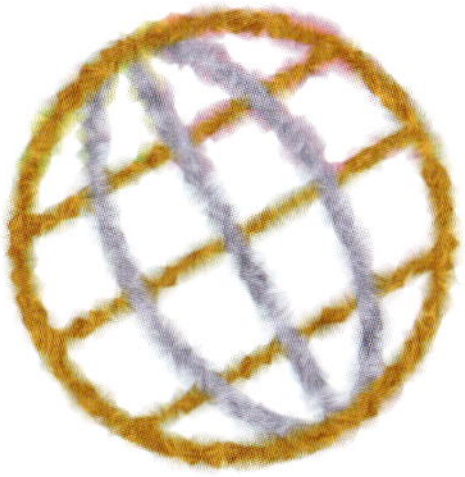

Swirl - Halva

Cutout

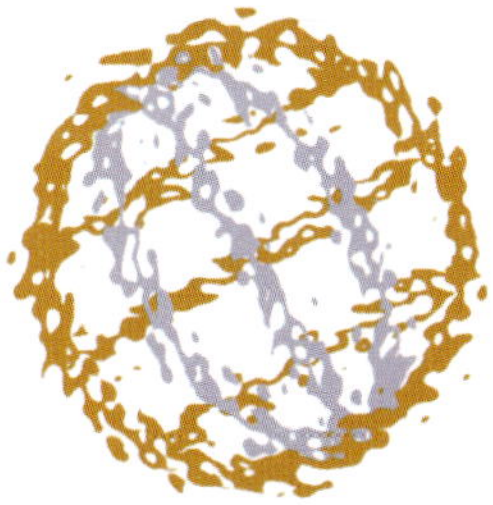

Jiggle - Tiny Bubbles

Carved - Smooth & Shiny

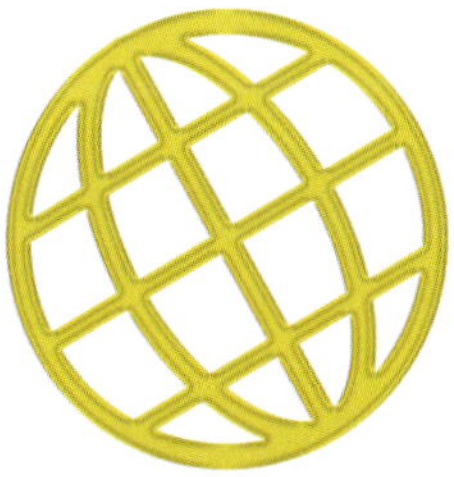

Chrome - Gold

Chrome - Mercury

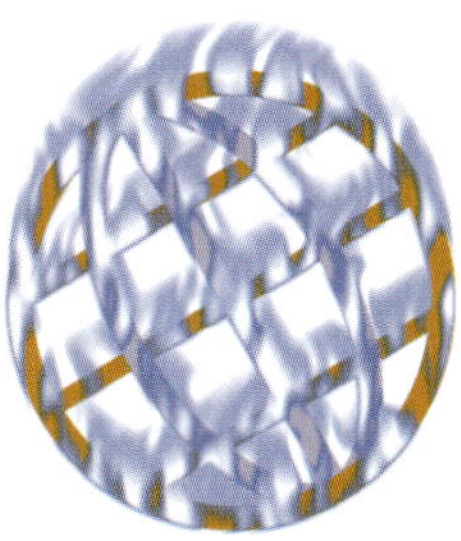

Flames - Lapping

Squint

## Macromedia FreeHand

Macromedia Freehand 7.0 is an extensive drawing program that can be utilized in multiple ways.

**CLARK PRODUCTIONS**

Client

*Bruce Clark Productions*

Design Firm

**Hornall Anderson Design Works**

Seattle, Washington

ARIZONA
ARTHRITIS
CENTER

Client
*Arizona Arthritis Center*
Design Firm
**Boelts Bros. Associates**
Tucson, Arizona

POLARIS
VENTURE PARTNERS

Client
*Polaris Venture Partners*
Design Firm
**Hansen Design Company**
Seattle, Washington

Smudge

Client
*Bugis Junction*
Design Firm
**Communication Arts Inc.**
Boulder, Colorado

BUGIS
JUNCTION

Client
*Journeys*
Design Firm
**Communication Arts Inc.**
Boulder, Colorado

Client

*Boelts Bros. 10th Anniversary*

Design Firm

**Boelts Bros. Associates**

Tucson, Arizona

Client

*Living Well*

Design Firm

**Boelts Bros. Associates**

Tucson, Arizona

Client

*Foster Brothers*

Design Firm

**Communication Arts Inc.**

Boulder, Colorado

ALKI BAKERY

Client
*Alki Bakery*
Design Firm
**Hornall Anderson Design Works**
Seattle, Washington

Client

*Ward Andrews Research in Design*

Design Firm

**Ward Andrews Research in Design**

Tucson, Arizona

This logo also utilized Adobe Photoshop.

Tweak

---

Skew Gradation

Client

*CNA Architecture*

Design Firm

**Hansen Design Company**

Seattle, Washington

Client

*McMahon*

Design Firm

**Boelts Bros. Associates**

Tucson, Arizona

Client

*Alta Beverage Company*

Design Firm

**Hornall Anderson Design Works**

Seattle, Washington

Client
*Cramer Calligraphy*
Design Firm
**Love Packaging Group**
Wichita, Kansas

Spiral

Client
*McCaw*
Design Firm
**Hornall Anderson Design Works**
Seattle, Washington

Client
*Grumpier Old Men softball team*
Design Firm
**conjoin**
Tucson, Arizona

Logo also utilized Adobe Photoshop and Adobe Illustrator.

Polygon Tweak

---

Client
*Nantucket Golf Club*
Design Firm
**Communication Arts Inc.**
Boulder, Colorado

Client
*Tenderfoot Lodge*
Design Firm
**Communication Arts Inc.**
Boulder, Colorado

Client
*Clayco*
Design Firm
**CUBE Advertising & Design**
St. Louis, Missouri

Client
*CW Wraps (Mondeo)*
Design Firm
**Hornall Anderson Design Works**
Seattle, Washington

Client
*Toll-Free Cellular*
Design Firm
**Hornall Anderson Design Works**
Seattle, Washington

Client

*Foster Pepper Shefelman*

Design Firm

**Hornall Anderson Design Works**

Seattle, Washington

Client

*Bugis Junction*

Design Firm

**Communication Arts Inc.**

Boulder, Colorado

PACIFIC PLACE

Client
*Pacific Place*
Design Firm
**Hornall Anderson Design Works**
Seattle, Washington

---

Client
*Ontario Mills*
Design Firm
**Communication Arts Inc.**
Boulder, Colorado

ONTARIO MILLS

Client

*Sun Tran Go Card*

Design Firm

**Boelts Bros. Associates**

Tucson, Arizona

Client

*The Library Ltd., bookstore*

Design Firm

**CUBE Advertising & Design**

St. Louis, Missouri

Client

*AOPA Fire Skull*

Design Firm

**Boelts Bros. Associates**

Tucson, Arizona

Client

*Starbucks Coffee Company*

Design Firm

**Hornall Anderson Design Works**

Seattle, Washington

Client
*Jamba Juice*
Design Firm
**Hornall Anderson Design Works**
Seattle, Washington

Client
*Game Creek Club*
Design Firm
**Communication Arts Inc.**
Boulder, Colorado

THE FRESHWATER GROUP

Client

*Freshwater Group*

Design Firm

**Boelts Bros. Associates**

Tucson, Arizona

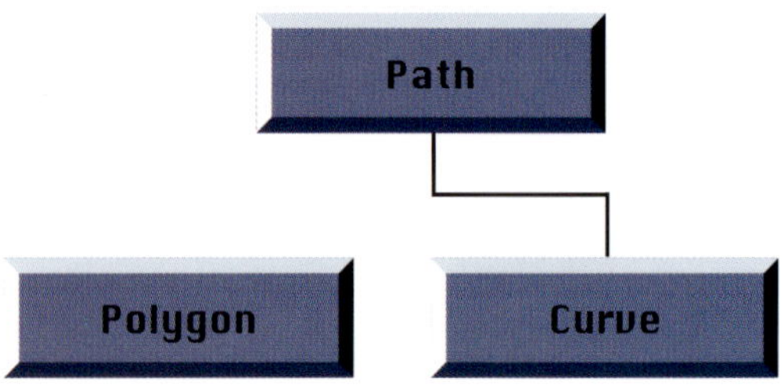


Client

*Hastings Filters Inc.*

Design Firm

**Love Packaging Group**

Wichita, Kansas

Logo also utilized Photoshop.

Client
*Rhino Chasers*
Design Firm
**Hornall Anderson Design Works**
Seattle, Washington

Client
*NextLink Corporation*
Design Firm
**Hornall Anderson Design Works**
Seattle, Washington

# Fontographer

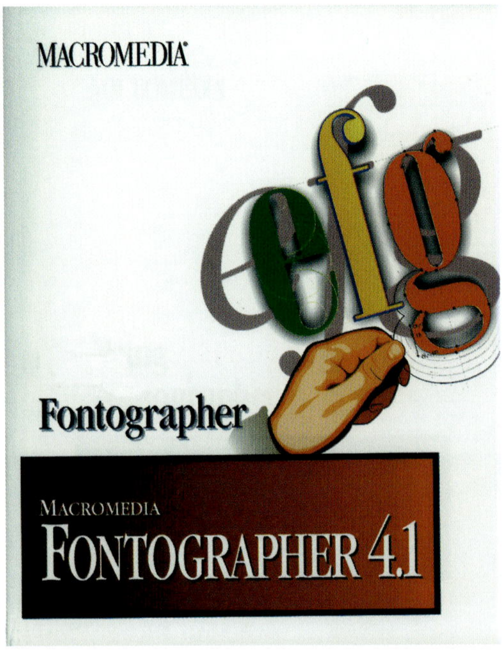


Macromedia Fontographer has a highly favorable reputation among people who design fonts, but it has a lot of utility for anyone who designs logos.

There are a couple of ways in which the logo creator might use Fontographer. The first is to create unusual alphabetic characters as a logo (or as a logo element). In the example below, the "f" on the left is the original character from an alphabet. On the right is a modified version of the same letter, which was done very quickly and precisely inside Fontographer. A second use is in the design of a complete font for exclusive use by a business. Many years ago, a "personal" font for a company was a huge luxury that was afforded only by deep-pocketed firms. Today, anyone can have a corporate font.

With Fontographer, you can create a corporate alphabet style to match your logo. The letters shown here all compliment the "A" logo. Within this program, you can modify letters, then create a font set by clicking the mouse.

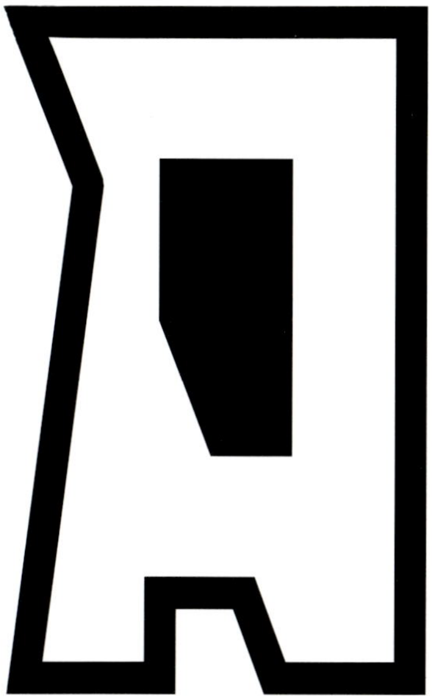

B D E F

H K L M

N P R U

Fontographer is a product of Macromedia, 600 Townsend, San Francisco, CA 94103. www.macromedia.com.

# CorelDRAW™

CorelDRAW™ was the dominant drawing program for the PC platform for many years, and still has a major share of the market. One reason for Corel's top position was that FreeHand and Illustrator did not have PC versions until somewhat recently. Don't assume, though, that CorelDRAW™ is so popular simply because there was no competition in the PC market. (Note to Mac users: CorelDRAW™ 6.0 is now available for the Macintosh platform.) Unlike many PC programs that appear with a Mac label,CorelDRAW™ has all the feel that Macintosh users have come to expect.

Simply stated, CorelDRAW™, Illustrator, and FreeHand have a lot of similar characteristics. As far as their ability as drawing tools, there's probably less than 10% difference among the three products.

Where CorelDRAW™ has a big edge on Illustrator and FreeHand is in the extras that come in the box. For example, CorelDRAW™ comes with more than 1,000 fonts, not to mention a chunk of quality stock photos and art.

You can't use a national flag or a shield as a logo (see using logo as clip art on page 145), but you can use parts of the design, or you may do substantial modifications. Anyway, the art below is just to show you the range of art available in CorelDRAW™.

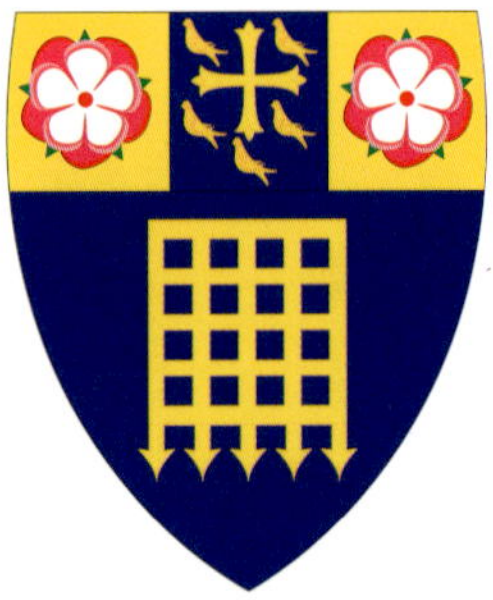

People who create identity systems along with their logos like to have a variety of fonts inside a family for various applications. The type collection inside CorelDRAW™ includes a much larger family than you'll find in most other places. Here, it takes up a full page just to show the entire Swiss 721 (a Helvetica® equivalent). If you were to buy this collection from a type house, it would cost somewhere in the range of $180 or so.

The font Swiss 721 may not be distributed electronically.

## Swiss 721

abcdefghijklmnopqrstuvwxyzABCDEFGHIJKLMNOPQRSTUVWYYZ1234567890&

*abcdefghijklmnopqrstuvwxyzABCDEFGHIJKLMNOPQRSTUVWYYZ1234567890&*

***abcdefghijklmnopqrstuvwxyzABCDEFGHIJKLMNOPQRSTUVWYYZ1234567890&***

abcdefghijklmnopqrstuvwxyzABCDEFGHIJKLMNOPQRSTUVWYYZ1234567890&

abcdefghijklmnopqrstuvwxyzABCDEFGHIJKLMNOPQRSTUVWYYZ1234567890&

*abcdefghijklmnopqrstuvwxyzABCDEFGHIJKLMNOPQRSTUVWYYZ1234567890&*

abcdefghijklmnopqrstuvwxyzABCDEFGHIJKLMNOPQRSTUVWYYZ12345

*abcdefghijklmnopqrstuvwxyzABCDEFGHIJKLMNOPQRSTUVWYYZ1234567890&*

**abcdefghijklmnopqrstuvwxyzABCDEFGHIJKLMNOPQRSTUVWYYZ1234567890&**

***abcdefghijklmnopqrstuvwxyzABCDEFGHIJKLMNOPQRSTUVWYYZ1234567890&***

abcdefghijklmnopqrstuvwxyzABCDEFGHIJKLMNOPQRSTUVWYYZ1234567890&

abcdefghijklmnopqrstuvwxyzABCDEFGHIJKLMNOPQRSTUVWYYZ1234567890&

*abcdefghijklmnopqrstuvwxyzABCDEFGHIJKLMNOPQRSTUVWYYZ1234567890&*

abcdefghijklmnopqrstuvwxyzABCDEFGHIJKLMNOPQRSTUVWYYZ123

**abcdefghijklmnopqrstuvwxyzABCDEFGHIJKLMNOPQRSTUVWYYZ1234567890**

**abcdefghijklmnopqrstuvwxyzABCDEFGHIJKLMNOPQRSTUVWYYZ1234567890&**

***abcdefghijklmnopqrstuvwxyzABCDEFGHIJKLMNOPQRSTUVWYYZ1234567890&***

abcdefghijklmnopqrstuvwxyzABCDEFGHIJKLMNOPQRSTUVWYYZ1234567890&

**abcdefghijklmnopqrstuvwxyzABCDEFGHIJKLMNOPQRSTUVWY**

***abcdefghijklmnopqrstuvwxyzABCDEFGHIJKLMNOPQRSTUVWYYZ1234567890&***

abcdefghijklmnopqrstuvwxyzABCDEFGHIJKLMNOPQRSTUVWYYZ1234567890&

**abcdefghijklmnopqrstuvwxyzABCDEFGHIJKLMNOPQRSTUVWYYZ1234567890&**

**abcdefghijklmnopqrstuvwxyzABCDEFGHIJKLMNOPQRSTUVWYYZ123**

**abcdefghijklmnopqrstuvwxyzABCDEFGHIJKLMNOPQRSTUVWYYZ12**

**abcdefghijklmnopqrstuvwxyzABCDEFGHIJKLMNOPQRSTUVWYYZ1234567890&**

***abcdefghijklmnopqrstuvwxyzABCDEFGHIJKLMNOPQRSTUVWYYZ1234567890&***

**abcdefghijklmnopqrstuvwxyzABCDEFGHIJKLMNOPQR**

***abcdefghijklmnopqrstuvwxyzABCDEFGHIJKLMNOPQRSTUVWYYZ12345***

abcdefghijklmnopqrstuvwxyzABCDEFGHIJKLMNOPQRSTUVWYYZ123

**abcdefghijklmnopqrstuvwxyzABCDEFGHIJKLMNOPQRSTUVWYYZ1234**

**abcdefghijklmnopqrstuvwxyzABCDEFGHIJKLMNOPQRSTUVWYYZ1234567**

***abcdefghijklmnopqrstuvwxyzABCDEFGHIJKLMNOPQRSTUVWYYZ12345678***

CorelDRAW™ includes a Corel TEXTURE™ module (Corel Artisian) which includes a number of backgrounds which can be very useful in the design process. For example, any of these backgrounds may be moved into a program such as Photoshop and changed at will.

One of the many features in CorelDRAW™ is Corel TEXTURE™, which has a number of different options. One of the ways you can work in this section is to import a design (logo, or whatever) and then use a variety of layers, lighting controls, colors, and backgrounds to create a neat graphic such as those shown below.

All of these designs started with the red "&" shown at right. All six were completed in a total of about 20 minutes. Very user friendly!

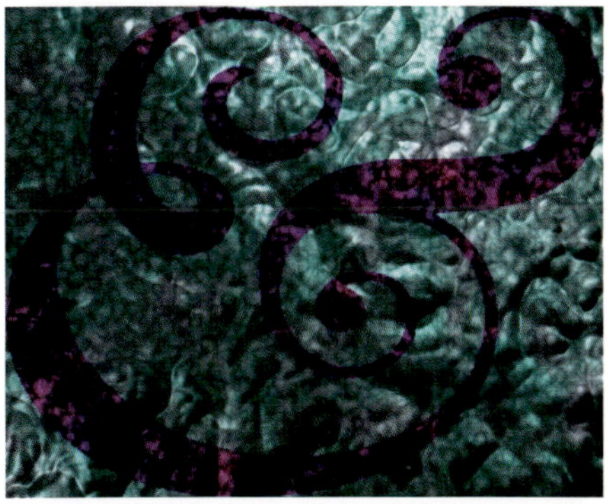

Corel Draw is a product of Corel Corporation, 1600 Carling Avenue, Ottawa, Ontario, Canada K1Z 8R7.

# Fractal Design Painter

Painter has everything a logo designer needs: a great variety of media, textured paper, colored paper and media, and a few big-name artists thrown in for good measure (Seurat, Van Gogh, and a nameless Impressionist). You can choose pencil weight, brush width, paint thickness, and in some cases, the condition of the brush or pen. Another interesting feature of Painter is the Image Hose. This feature lets you "spray" an image onto the canvas through different "nozzles." These nozzles have spray handprints, clouds, ivy, flowers, and forests in different sizes and spray patterns. The more you work with this product, the more neat features you'll discover. Remember the fun you had with super Spirograph and Etch-a-Sketch? Multiply that by 1,000 and you get some idea of how much you'll enjoy using Fractal Design Painter.

Artist Pastel Chalk

Big Wet Oils

Thick & Thin

Felt Marker

Thick Oil

Thick & Thin Pencil

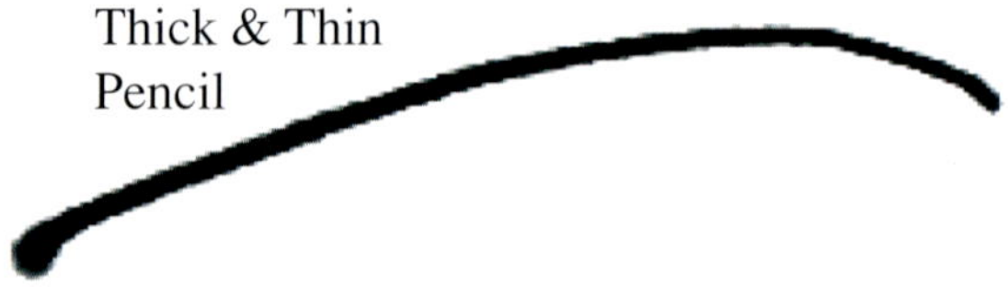

Driving Rain Cloner

Big Dry Ink - Splatter

Dirty Marker

Oil Paint

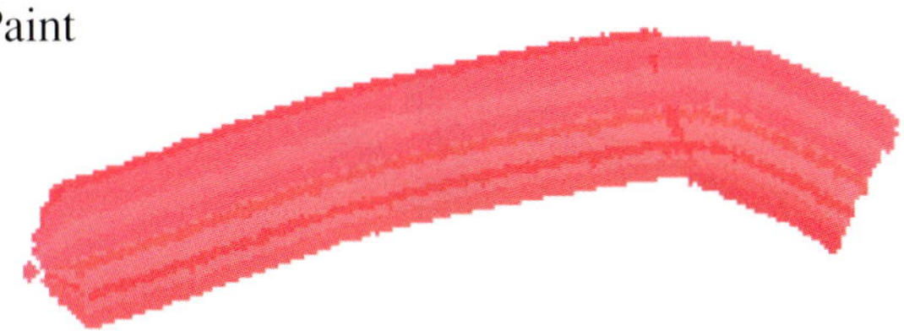

Oil F

Big Dry Ink

Seurat

Simple Water

Digital Sumi

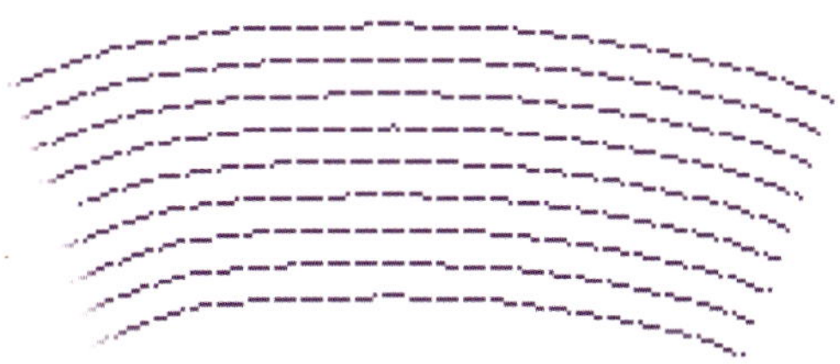

2B Pencil

Soft Charcoal

Spatter Water

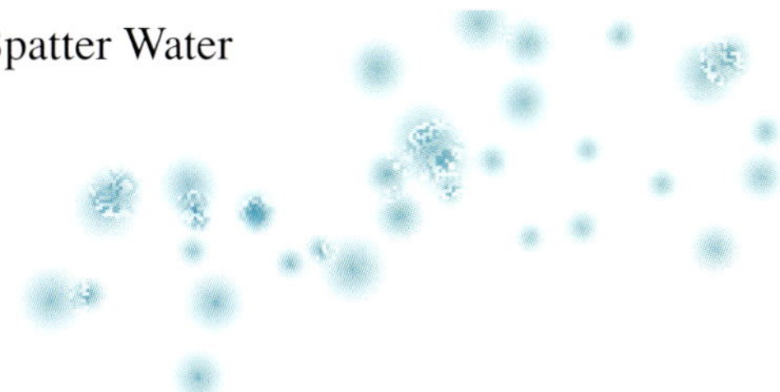

Square Chalk

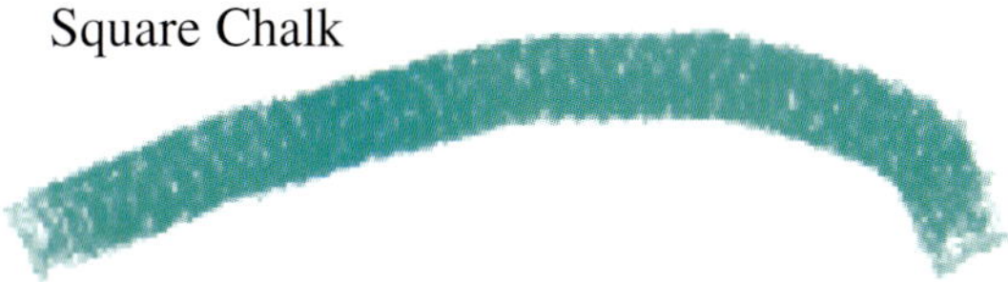

Liquid Total Oil Brush

Fat Stroke Airbrush

Leaky Pen

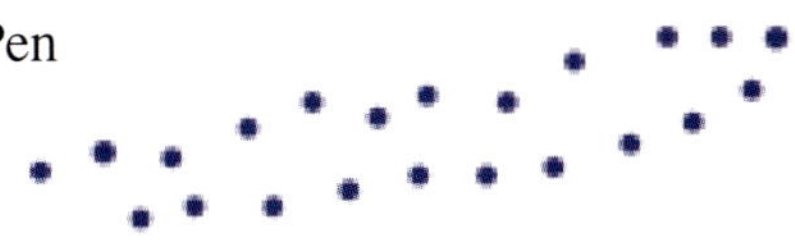

Big Dry Ink

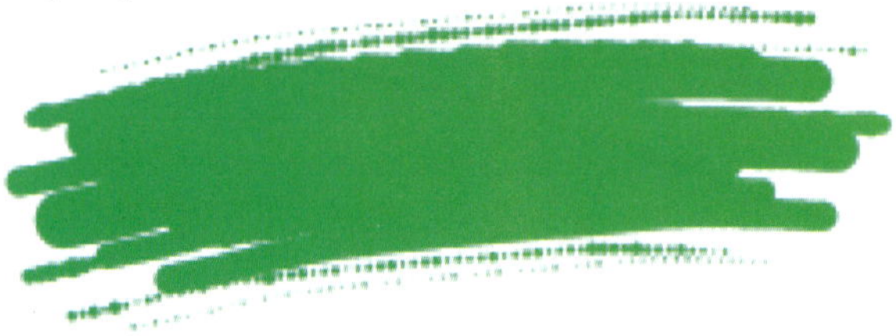

Hairy Brush

Penetration Brush

Thin Stroke Airbrush

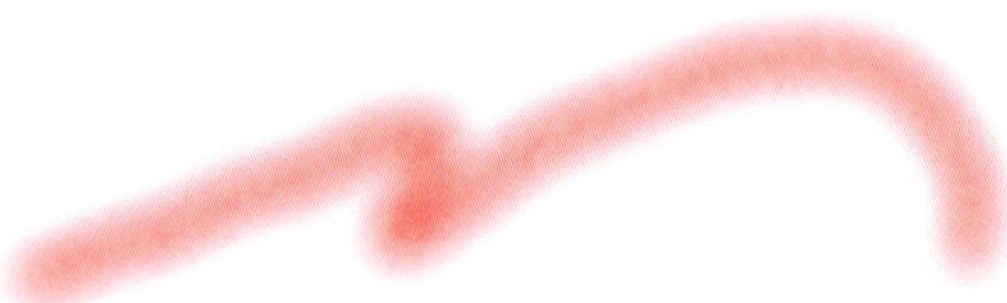

Coarse Smeary Bristles

Scratchboard Tool

Pens - Flat Color

Large Chalk

Camel Hair Brush

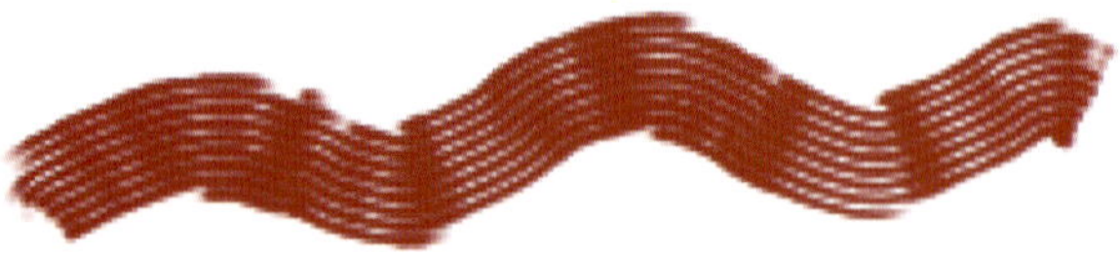

Single Pixel Scribbler

Colored Pencils

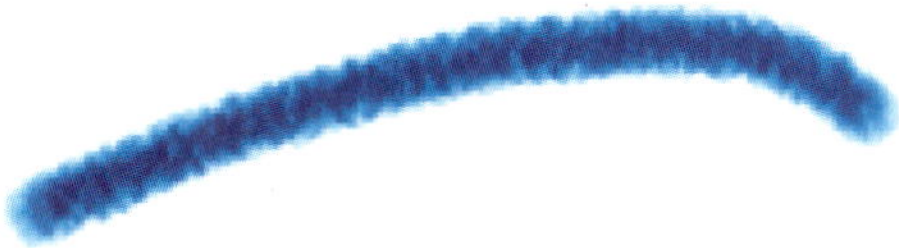

Spatter Airbrush

Scratch Board Rake

Cover Brush

Big Wet Luscious

Huge Rough Out

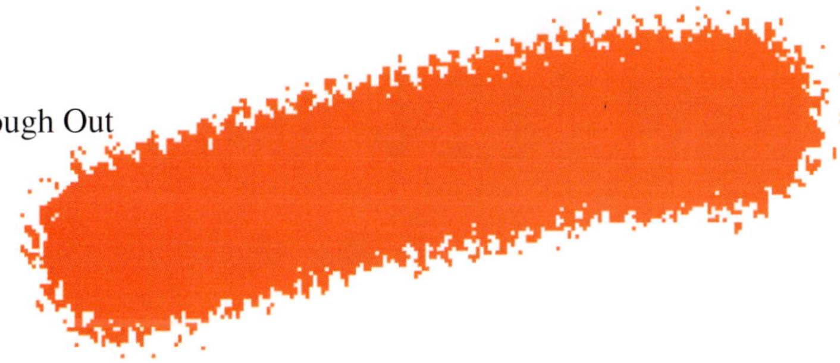

Chalk on Hatching

Crayon on Ribbed Pastel

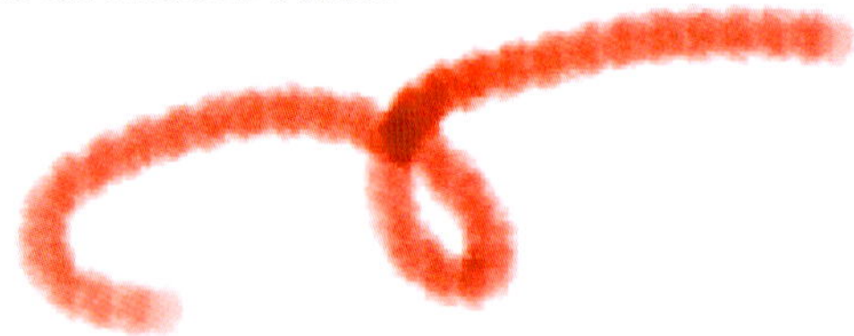

Soft Charcoal - Handmade Paper

Palette Knife

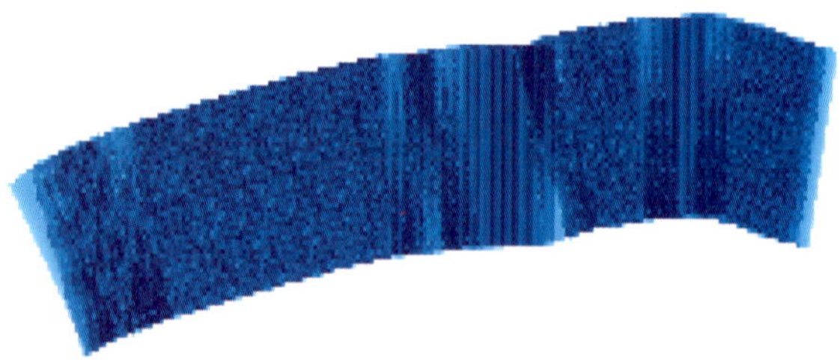

Image Hose: Small Random Spray - English Ivy

Image Hose: Small Random Linear - Handprints

Image Hose: Small Luminance - Poppies

Image Hose: Small Luminance - Poppies

Mouse Rubber Stamp with Pattern

Fractal Design Painter 5 is a product of Meta Creations Corporation, 5550 Scotts Valley Drive, Scotts Valley, CA 95066. Sales and product information: (800) 677-7388. www.fractal.com.

# Multi-Ad Creator 2

Multi-Ad Creator seems like any other page layout program when you open it, but its capabilities seem to go far beyond most. Aside from the regular layout function of the program, you can draw and easily manipulate fairly detailed artwork.

Creator also lets you fill shapes with different textures, such as clouds and leopard-print.

Asian Sunrise

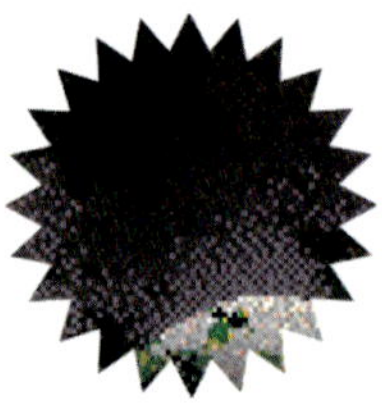

Fernbar

Greencloud

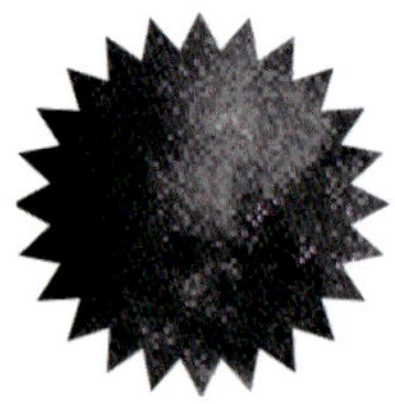

Forest

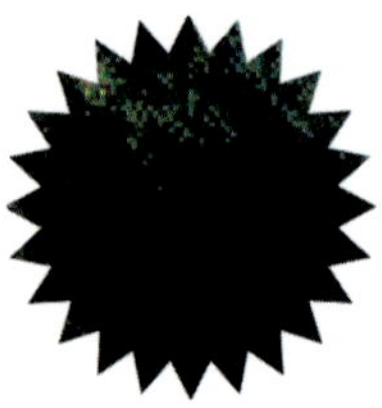

Jungle

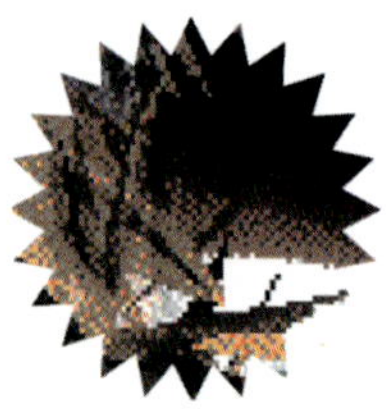

Fractal World

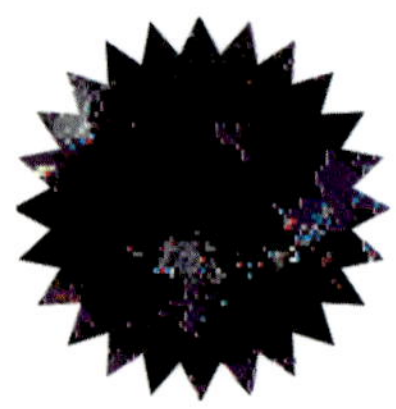

Magenta Shag

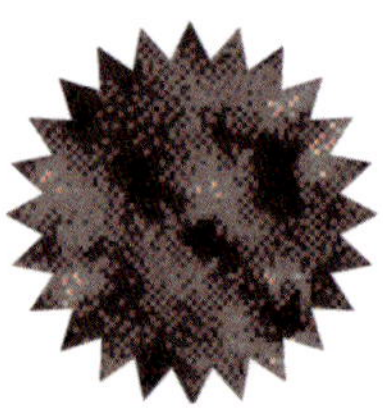

Nebula

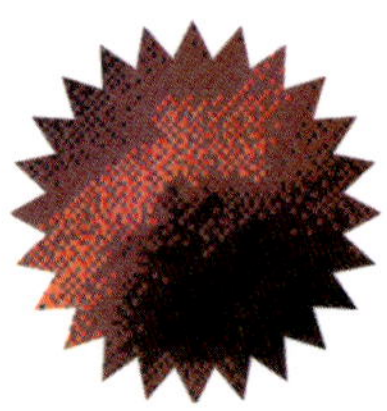

Mauve & Blue

Pastel

Spaced Out

Midnight

Purple Leopard

Tarnish

RGB

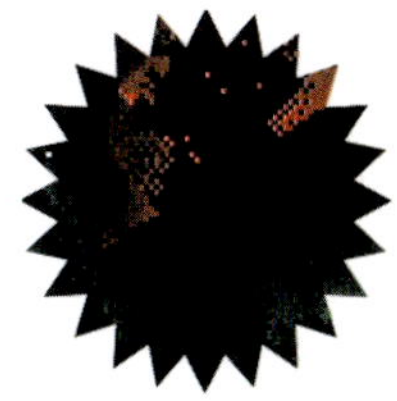

Multi-Ad Creator 2 is a product of Multi-Ad Services, Inc., 1720 West Detweiller Drive, Peoria, IL 61615-1695. Phone: (309) 692-1530. www.multi-ad.com.

# Fractal Design Expression

This software has recently become my favorite toy. (Note that I use "toy" in a most respectful sense of the word.) Expression has a wonderful feature in which the character of a stroke can be changed just by a click of the mouse. A module called "Stroke Warehouse" has hundreds of predefined stroke styles which emulate various pencils, brushes, and more. You can also control each stroke's thickness, etc. with slider controls which let you see changes as they happen.

This is just one feature of Expression, but it's so powerful (and easy) that I decided to devote four pages to just showing how a basic stroke can be changed into many variations. This program will change the way you design logos, and give you many new techniques to use as you create.

**Basic Line**

Aged Brush

Big Ink

Brushed Ink

Comet

Crow Quill 1

Crow Quill 2

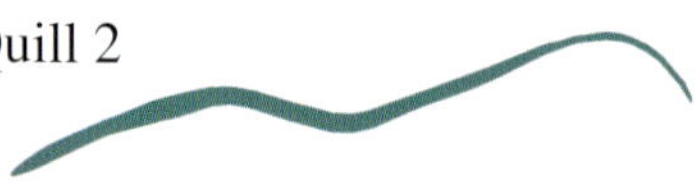

Dabbed

Fanned

Generic

Gradpen

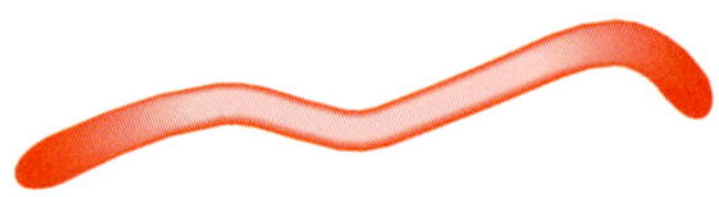

India Ink

Ink on Sable

Leaky

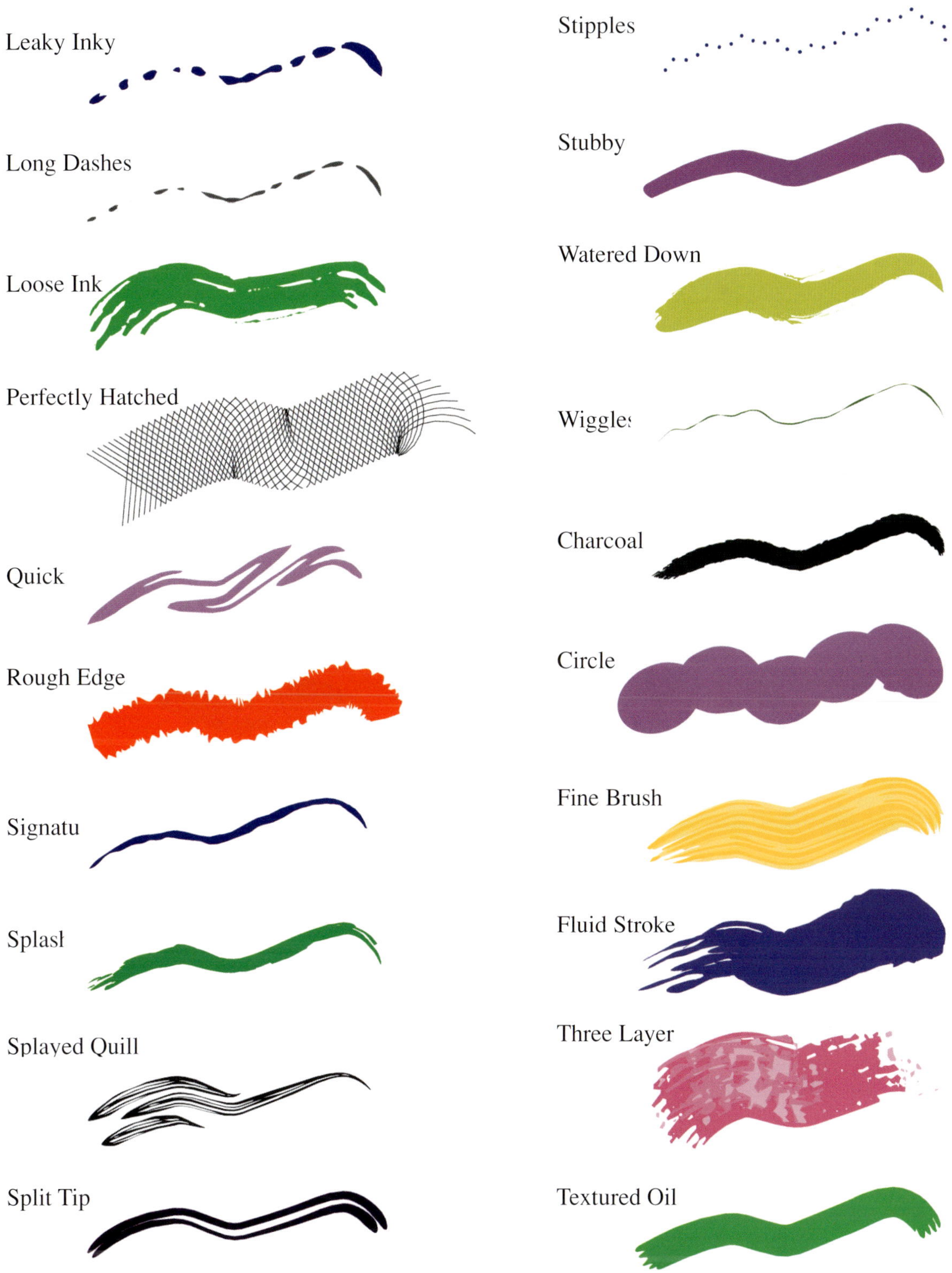
Leaky Inky
Long Dashes
Loose Ink
Perfectly Hatched
Quick
Rough Edge
Signatu
Splas
Splayed Quill
Split Tip
Stipples
Stubby
Watered Down
Wiggle
Charcoal
Circle
Fine Brush
Fluid Stroke
Three Layer
Textured Oil

This Air

Thin to Thick

Tire Tracks

Water Brush

Wide Taper

Brush Pen

Dotted Line

Dotty

Fading Ends

Fine Soft Bristle

Fine Tip

Finger Paint

Flat Brush

Heavy Pen

Highlighter

Medium Sable

Pillar

Pointed

Pointed Leaf

Soft Edged Marker

Solid Cover

Blended Rainbow

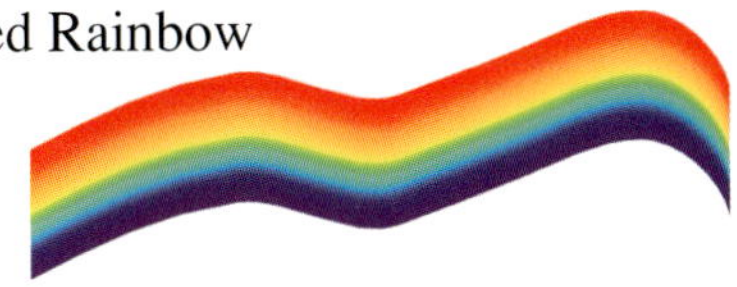

Textured Pen

Thin Middle

Leaf

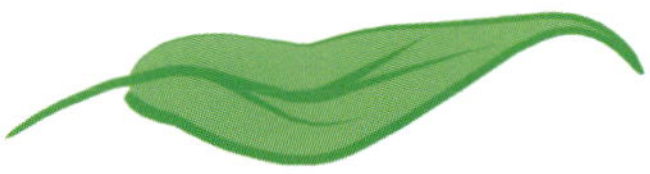

Purple Paper Snake

Spiralling branch

Splattered Edges

USflame 5

Bamboo Shoots

In addition to the many stroke styles, there are a number of "specialty" graphics which are also accessed simply by clicking the mouse. The group below is typical of these unusual elements.

Piano Keys

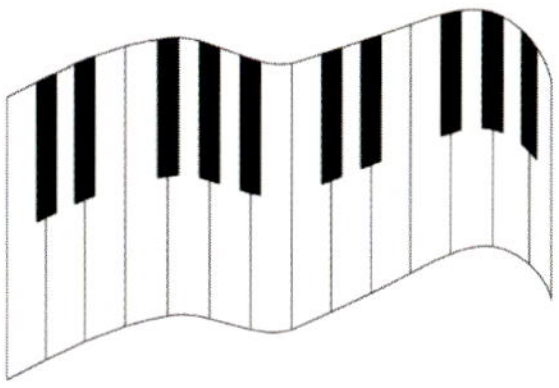

Plume

Kio

Human Footprints

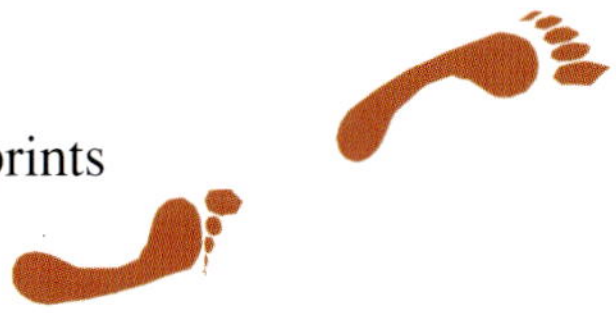

Hazard Tape

Arrow Splash

Film

Braided Rainbow

Fractal Design Expression is available from Meta Creations, 6303 Carpinteria Ave., Carpinteria, CA 93103
Phone: (800) 433-7732.

# Wild River SSK

Wild River SSK is a series of 7 Photoshop Filters; the modules are Chameleon, DekoBoko, MagicCurtain, Magic Frame, MagicMask, TileMaker, and TV Snow.

This design uses two Wild River SSK filters: the Deko-Boko was applied to get the beveled look, then the TV snow was added to get the lines.

Boko

Deko

Magic Frame

Magic Mask: License Plate effect

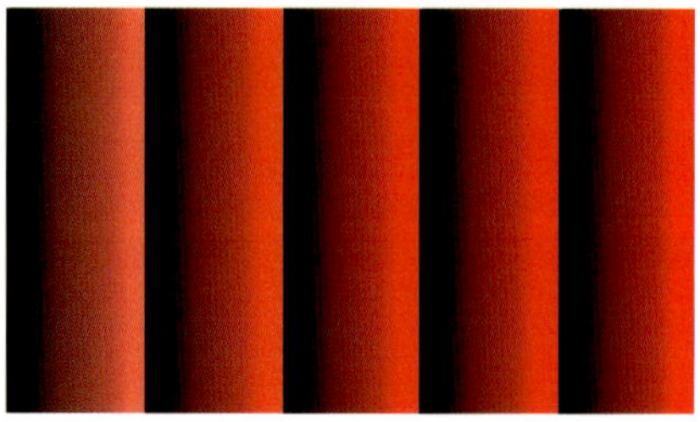

Magic Curtain

Wild River SSK has a highly powerful feature called "Magic Mask." There are 24 filters in this module that produce a wide range of graphic effects on type, or graphic objects.

The illustration here shows the screen, with the various slider controls that give the user even more flexibility in creating unusual effects.

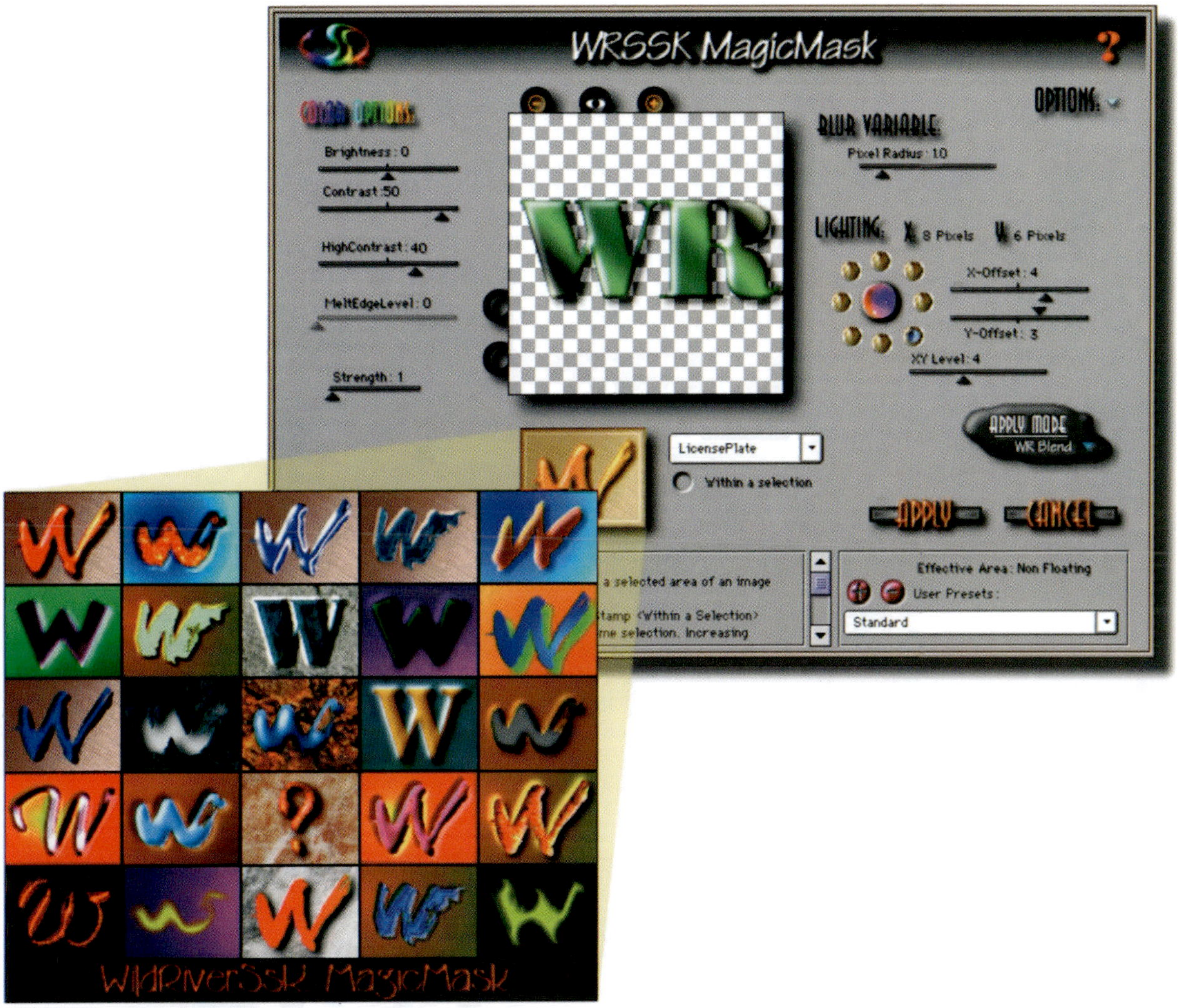


Wild River SSK is available from InTown Graphics, 814 Glendover Cove, Lexington, KY 40502.
Phone for orders: (203) 626-7779. Fax: (213) 621-2908.

# Vertigo 3D Hot Text

Vertigo 3D HotTEXT™ is an easy way to bring real 3D text and paths into Adobe Photoshop. You create 3D text, position it along a path, then add the 3D text to your Photoshop document with the click of a mouse.

HotTEXT has multiple control options so you can change the path, angle, depth, color, lighting and other features of dimensional text elements. It's all very simple with easily-followed on-screen help boxes to let you create unusual dimensional type in a minute or two.

clouds surface

neon surface

sunflower surface

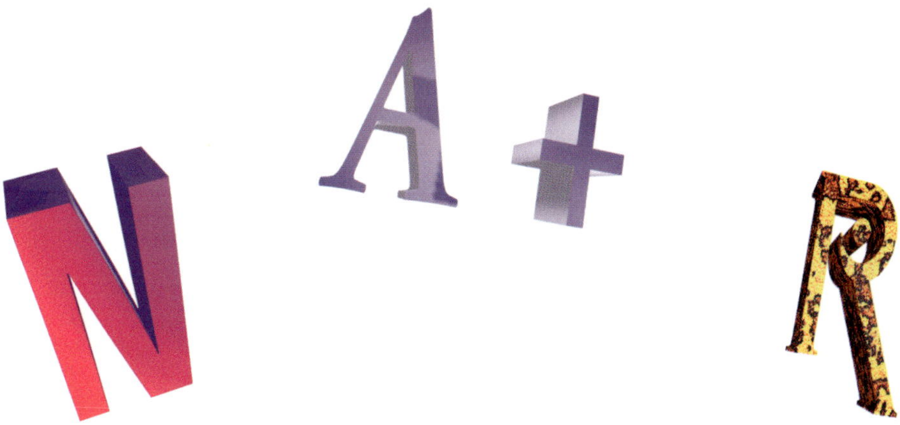


Vertigo 3D Dizzy is available from Vertigo Technology Inc., 1255 West Pender St., Vancouver, BC Canada V6E 2V1. Phone: (604) 684-2113. Fax: (604) 684-2108. www.vertigo3d.com

# Vertigo 3D Words

Vertigo 3D Words is a fast, efficient way to put real 3D text along 3D paths without leaving Adobe Illustrator. You can use your existing font library and create 3D type while using the many controls within this system. The easy-to-use interface shows you what the graphic looks like as you make changes in position, color, depth, and other specifications. Once you have the 3D Words document you want, you can then integrate with other graphics, as was done to create the "Sanibel" logo on the opposite page.

Vertigo 3D Dizzy is available from Vertigo Technology Inc., 1255 West Pender St., Vancouver, BC Canada V6E 2V1. Phone: (604) 684-2113. Fax: (604) 684-2108. www.vertigo3d.com

# Vertigo 3D Dizzy

Vertigo 3D Dizzy is used in conjunction with either Adobe Photoshop or Adobe Illustrator. With the click of a mouse, you get 3D effects immediately. In addition, you can add lighting effects, and a "virtual camera" lets you pick the exact angle you want.

The designs shown are typical of what can be accomplished with Vertigo 3D Dizzy.

Vertigo 3D Dizzy is available from Vertigo Technology Inc., 1255 West Pender St., Vancouver, BC Canada V6E 2V1. Phone: (604) 684-2113. Fax: (604) 684-2108. www.vertigo3d.com

# Ottopaths

Ottopaths is sold as an add-on filter for Photoshop. It actually works as a program within a program allowing you to create, flow, and warp text and shapes as paths.

Ottopaths is available from The Human Software Company, 19925 Stevens Creek Boulevard, Cupertino, CA 95014-2358. Phone: (408) 399-0057. Fax: (408) 399-0157. Website: www.humansoftware.com. E-mail: OTTO@humansoftware.com.

# Textissimo

Textissimo is an add-on text filter for Photoshop filled with hundreds of effects to apply to text. It also allows you to create personalized effects and add them to the Library.

Textissimo is available from The Human Software Company, 19925 Stevens Creek Boulevard, Cupertino, CA 95014-2358. Phone: (408) 399-0057. Fax: (408) 399-0157. Website: www.humansoftware.com.

# Andromeda Series Filters - Photography

The Andromeda Photography filters allow the user various effects with art **or** photographs. All effects on these two pages were the results of different filters used on the original star at bottom left.

# Andromeda Series Filters - 3D

The 3D filter in the Andromeda system allows the user to wrap graphics, photos, type, etc. around a sphere, plane, cylinder, or cube. The multiple controls allow adjustments to be made to the position, lighting, size, and other features of the design. The checkerboard grid below is shown as it is applied to the sphere at right.

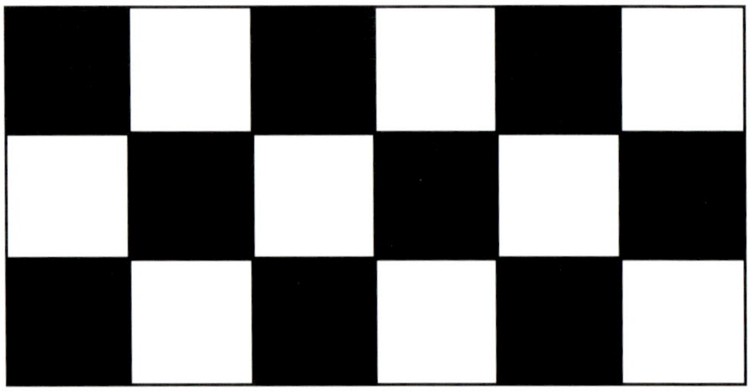

At right, the star is shown in different sizes. Directly below, the star is applied to a cube. The two designs at bottom right were processed with additional Photoshop filters: pointillize and ripple. When you use Photoshop filters, remember that you can get striking visuals by using multiple filters, one at a time.

Pointillize

Ripple

These examples show how the 3-D Andromeda Filter lets you control various factors in the final design.

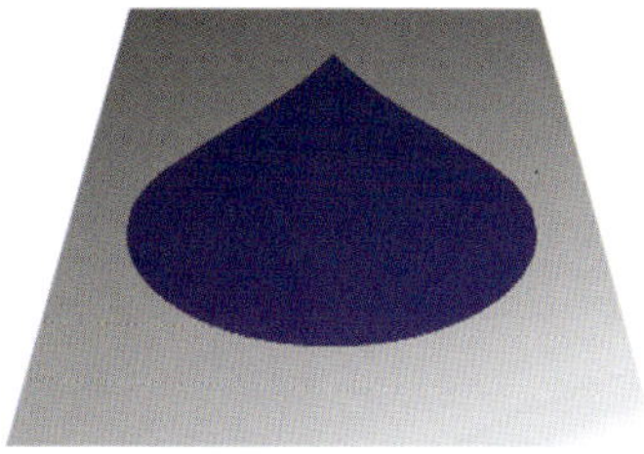
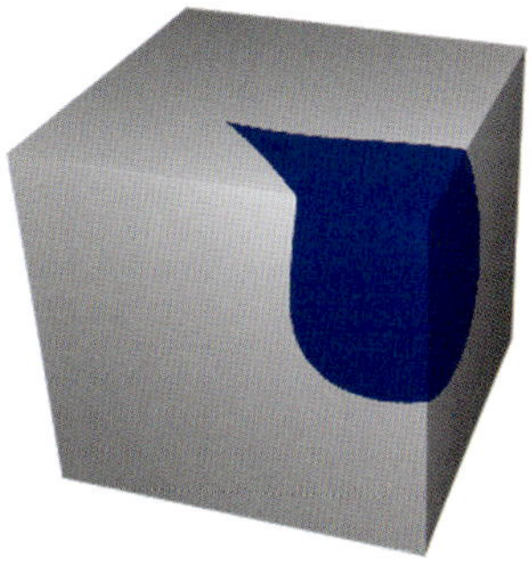
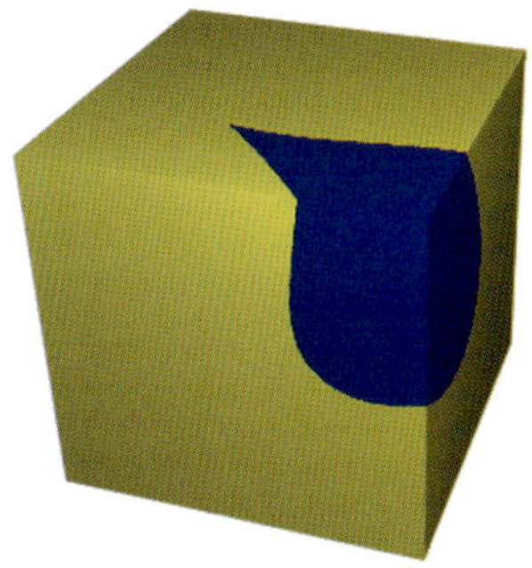
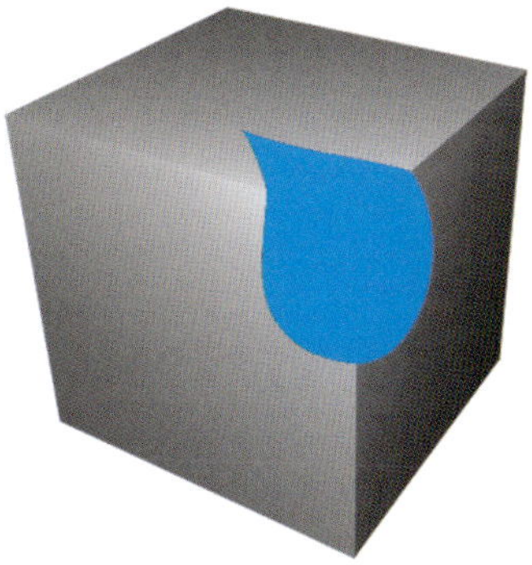

Cylinder Mode

Multiple Drops

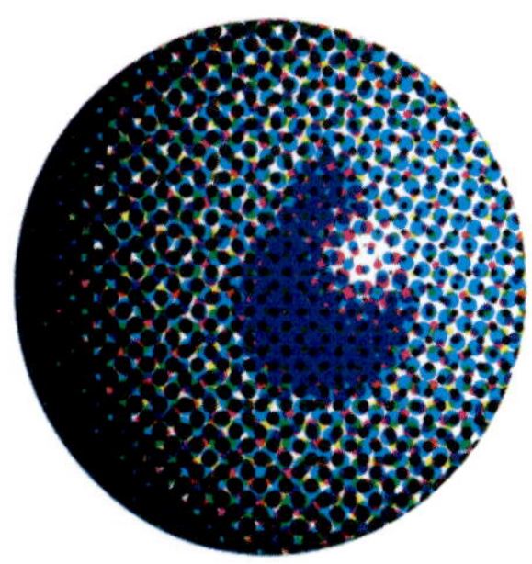

Additional Photoshop Filter

Andromeda Series Filters are products of Andromeda Software Inc., 699 Hampshire Road, Westlake Village, CA 91361. Phone: (805) 379-4109.

# Ray Dream 3D

Ray Dream 3D allows you to create nearly any object in three dimensions, with a variety of finishes: metal, wood, marble, and more. Ray Dream includes several different shape tools, as well as a free form tool to create your own shapes. It also includes some pre-existing artwork. Using different cameras views, you see your object from different angles.

Ambrosia

Brick-O!

Bark

Baseball

Brick-O!Bump

Chrome

Brushed

Faux-SMTPE]

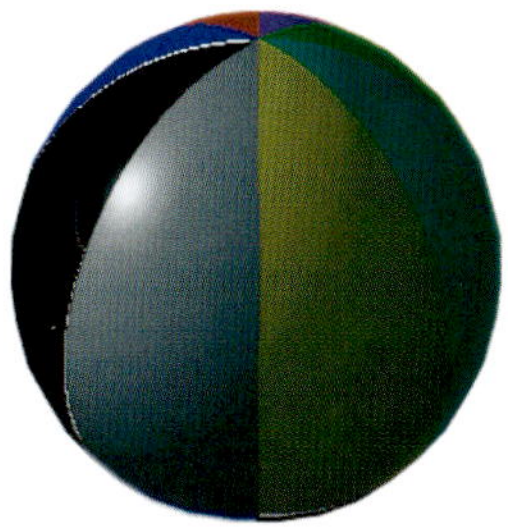

Checkers

Green

Chianti

Industrial Inci

Light

Oak-Brow

Marble

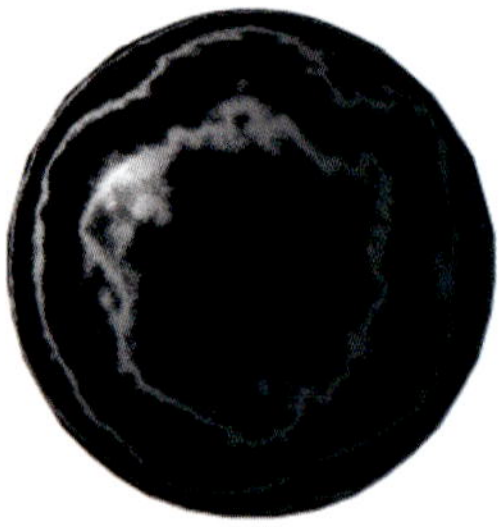

Orange-Veined Marble

Marble II

Polished

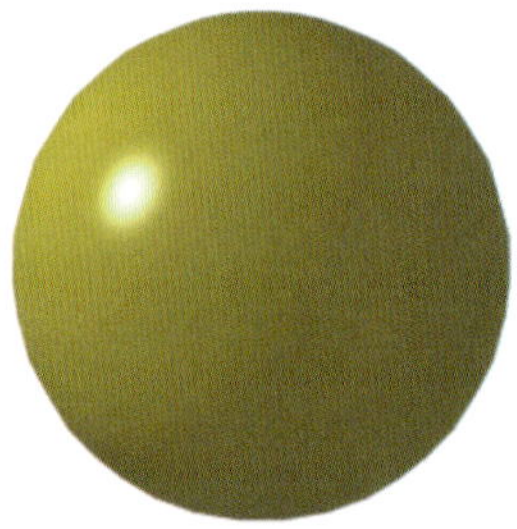

Nog 'n' Hide

Rosewood

Sand Blast

Tennis Ball

Silver

Wire Earth

Woody

Wood I

Red Metal

Veneer

# Specular LogoMotion

LogoMotion is an easy-to-use 3-D modeling program. While a lot of 3-D software is difficult to learn, LogoMotion's excellent instruction manual takes you through the steps easily and simply. The fact is, this might be seen as 3-D for beginners. (The same company makes Infini-D, a professional 3-D tool.)

LogoMotion lets you use type or objects such as graphics, icons, or logos to create flying images. There are also many stock backgrounds—such as the spotlight opposite—that you can insert with the click of a mouse. And, by simply saving any frame as a PICT or TIFF file, you can transfer the image into print, as we have done with the designs on these pages.

Specular LogoMotion is available from Meta Creations, 6303 Carpinteria Ave., Carpinteria, CA 93103. Phone: (800) 433-7732.

# Minicad 7

MiniCAD is a high-end design program that is used extensively by product designers, engineers, architects, drafters, and others who need the precision of multi-decimal accuracy.

Even though this program allows extremely precise rendering of dimensional products and even home models, it is still highly effective for designing corporate graphics.

The samples here show how the dimensionality can be used to create unusual effects.

The graphics below show how a sphere can be viewed from several different angles.

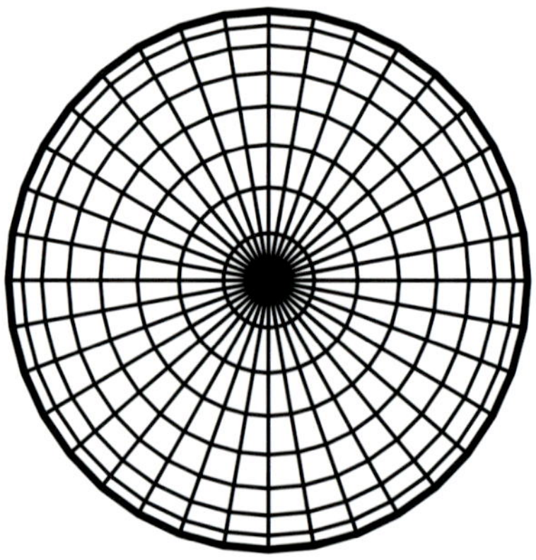

Top View

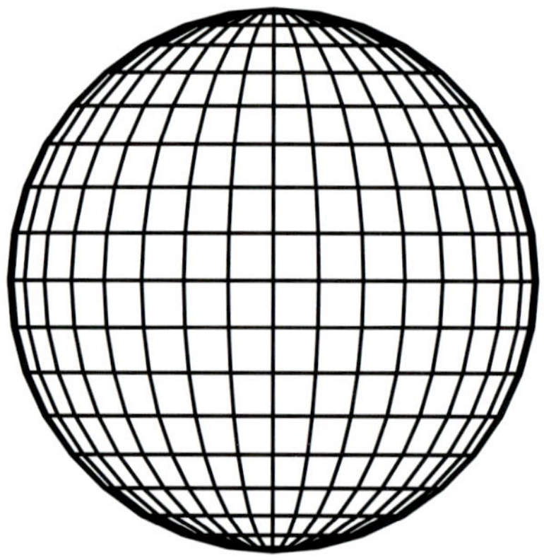

Front View

Right Isometric

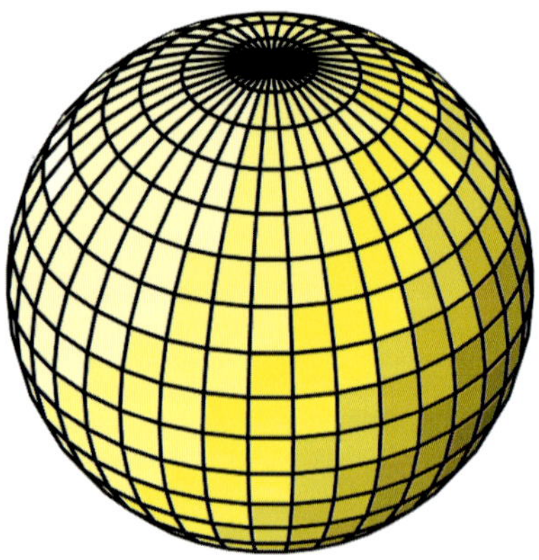

3-D Solid

Some of the shapes that can be easily produced in MiniCAD are shown here in Wireframe format.

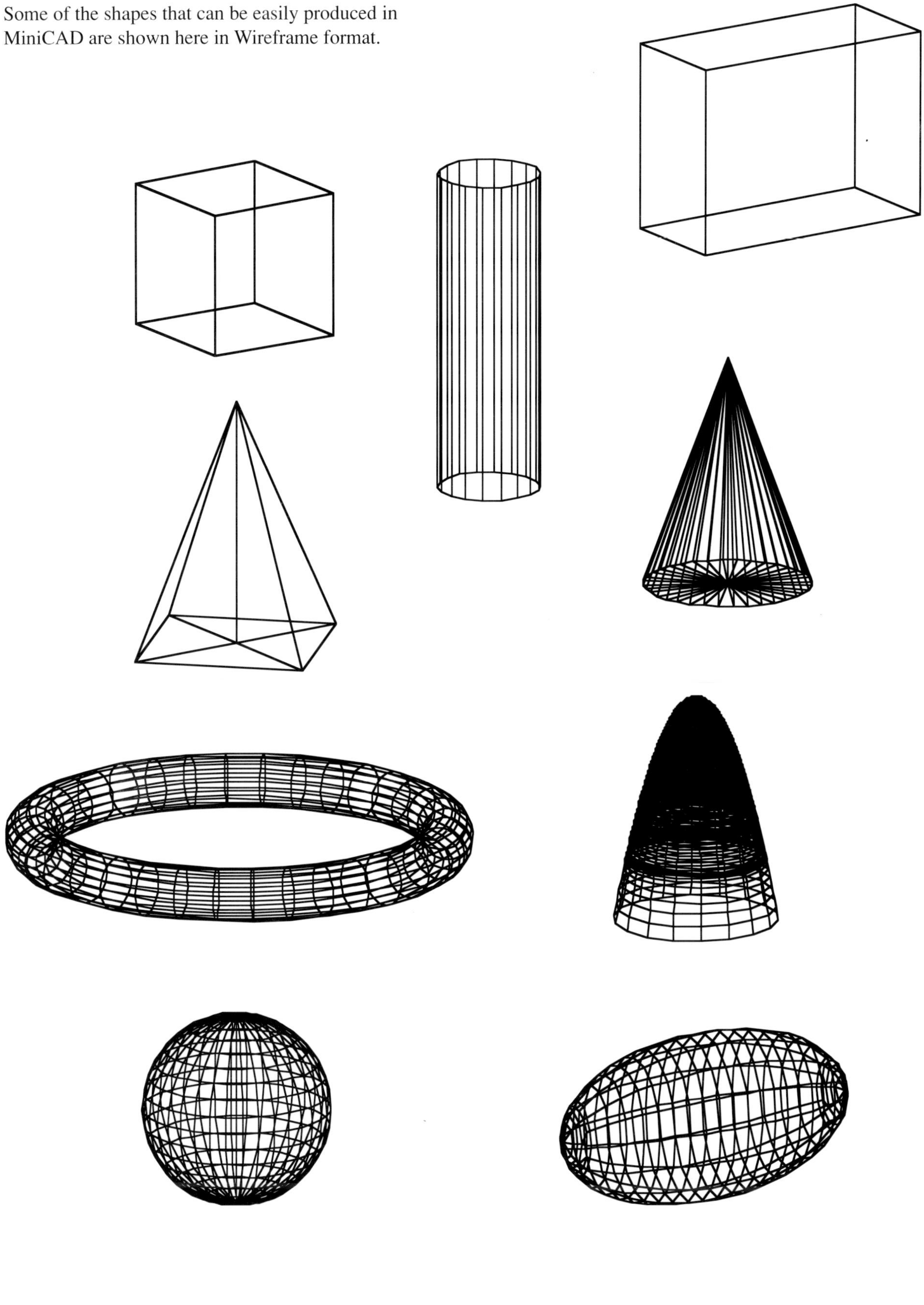

A sphere and a cone were rendered with the "Shaded, no lines" command to get the look here.

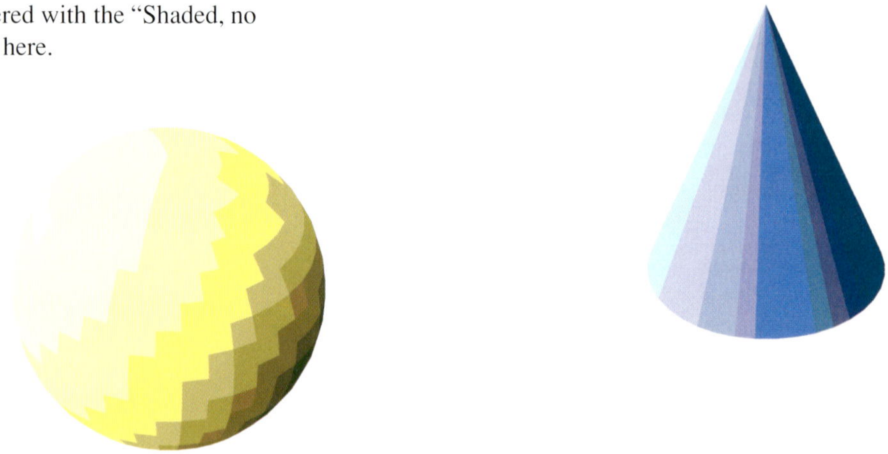

The cone was moved closer to the sphere. Note how the cone actually intersects into the sphere.

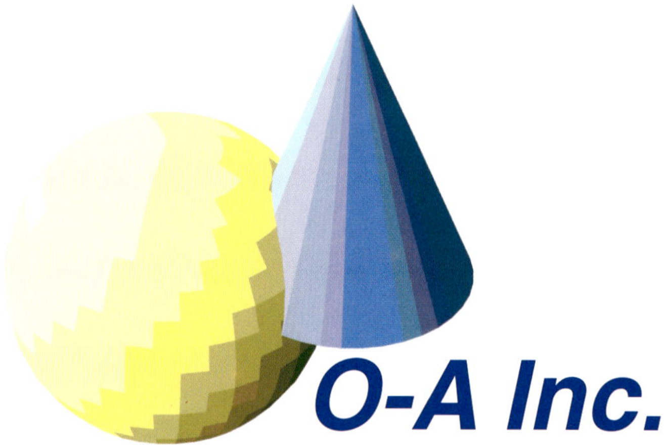


We changed the configuration so that the cone was behind the sphere. The design was then rendered with the "Render: QuickDraw 3D" command. The result is a more evenly polished look. (This design could easily be exported into Photoshop and treated with a filter to create a very distinctive look.)

The logo at the bottom of the opposite page was done with the perspective being the "Right Isometric" view. Here are three different views that are changed with the click of a mouse.

Lower left ISO

Lower Right ISO

Head-On

MiniCAD®7 is a product of Diehl Graphsoft, Inc., 10270 Old Columbia Road, Columbia, MD 21046-1751. Phone: (410) 290-5114. Fax: (410) 290-8050. Internet: www.diehlgraphsoft.com

# form•Z

form•Z is a very powerful program for solid and surface modeling. Quite simply, this program has the finest output capabilities of any product that I have seen with off-the-shelf availability.

The only drawback to form•Z is that it has so many complex features that it doesn't let you "open the box and work without reading the manual" like so many creative people like to do.

However, the potential that lies inside the box is well worth the time it takes to learn to use this product. The designs on the next six pages come from the samples folder on the program CD, so they were done by experienced people. However, this gives you an idea of what you'll be able to do with form•Z.

1995
Chardon
Quality Seal · Taster's Choice Award ·
Red Table Wine
Net 24 FL.OZ
Alcohol 11.8%

form·Z
RenderZone

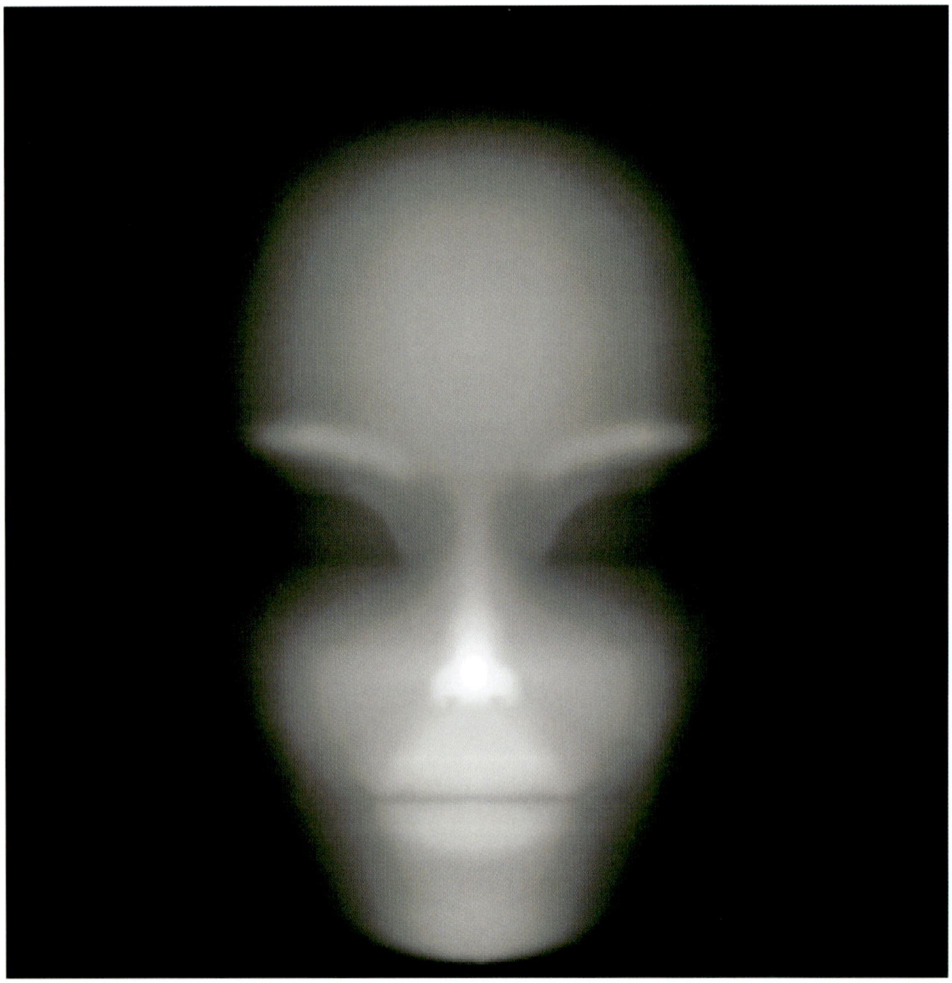

form•Z is a product of autodessy inc., 2011 Riverside Drive, Columbus, OH 43221. Phone: (614) 488-9777. Fax: (614) 488-0848. Internet: www.formz.com. e-mail: formZ@autodessy.com.

# Logo SuperPower

Logo SuperPower® is not a program, but a large database of more than 2,000 "design elements" which can opened and manipulated in drawing applications such as FreeHand, Illustrator, or Corel Draw. The examples below show how the product works. On the facing page are five logos which were created using a drawing program and Logo SuperPower elements. This product was created by David E. Carter, author of this book.

## How Logo SuperPower Works - Example 1

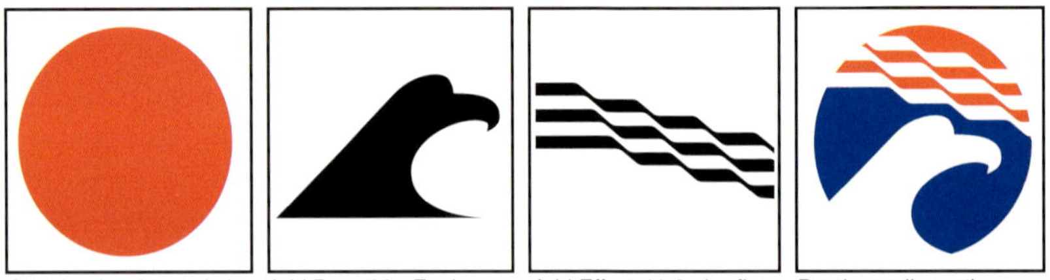

Start by drawing a circle (from the toolbox).

Add Base 86 - Eagle Head. Change it to white.

Add Effect 41-3, the flat wave. Change it to white. Then change its shape slightly.

Put them all together, change part of the circle to blue, and you have a great logo — in minutes.

## How Logo SuperPower Works - Example 2

Start with Base 16, the Water Drop.

Add Effect 08-3 (top). Delete two lines, then change shape of the remaining line (bottom).

Turn effect to white. Put it on top of water drop. (Shape is outlined here to show it fully.)

Copy effect and put in on top of water drop several times. Another great design in minutes.

## A small sample of the 2,000+ "design elements"

Logo SuperPower® is available from Decathlon Corp., 4100 Executive Park Drive, #16, Cincinnati, OH 45241.
Orders: (800) 648-5646. Questions: (606) 329-0077. Fax: (606) 329-0077. e-mail: creativitycenter@wwd.net

# Ultimate ID Manual

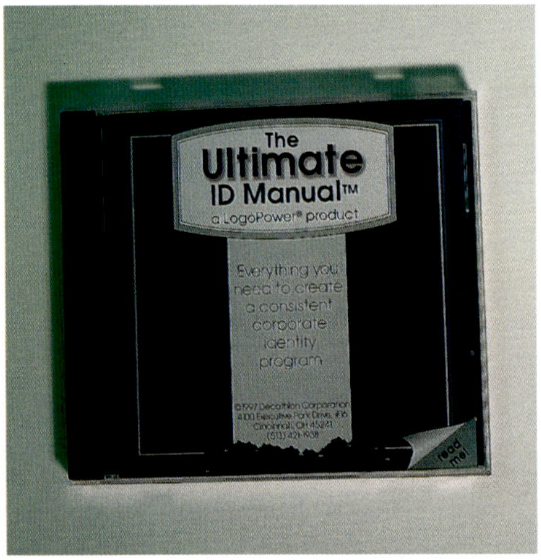


When you design a logo, the way it appears when it is *used* is a most important factor. In addition, the consistent usage of the logo is crucial to the logo's success as a marketing tool. The Ultimate ID Manual has more than 350 templates of items such as vehicles, signage, clothing, promotional items, etc. With this product, you can use just one for presentation, or you can make a highly detailed corporate identity manual using many of the templates. This product was created by David E. Carter, author of this book.

Healthy Stuff

Star Co.

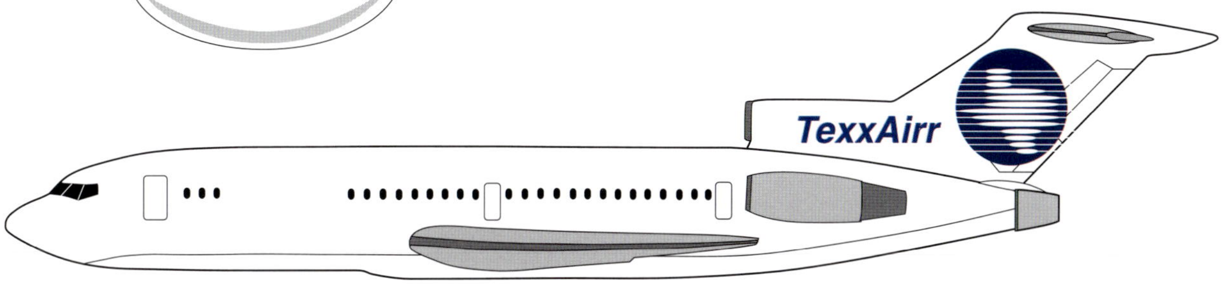
TexxAirr

# Specular Collage

Specular Collage is an easy-to-work-with program that allows you to manipulate high resolution images and text incorporating the final project into one piece. One of the strengths of this product is the minimal amount of time it takes to use. There's no endless waiting for artwork to recompose with every move or change because the initial collage uses only screen proxies. When a collage is finished, the user then renders it to a specified size and resolution. This can take a few minutes, but it's well worth the time (and aggravation) saved during creation.

Incorporating two or more images into a logo in Specular Collage is a snap. With one click on the "mask" option, pesky white backgrounds, which plague other programs, disappear.

(Type on paths was executed in Macromedia Freehand.)

Specular Collage is a product of Specular International, Ltd., 479 West Street, Amherst, MA 01002. Phone: (413) 253-3100.

# Adobe Streamline

Adobe Streamline is a highly useful tool which lets you quickly convert anyt black-and-white bitmapped or color pixel image into high-quality PostScript™ language line art. Once the art has been converted, you get access to the "points" and can edit the image any way you choose. With Streamline, you can open an image, or scan a photo, logo or whatever, and then easily make modifications.

This example shows how Adobe Streamline may be used effectively in the creation of logos. For the starting point, let's say you created a pencil sketch of the illustration at right. Maybe you don't have the computer skills yet to create this in a drawing program; simply scan it. Then, open the illustration in Streamline. (See opposite page.)

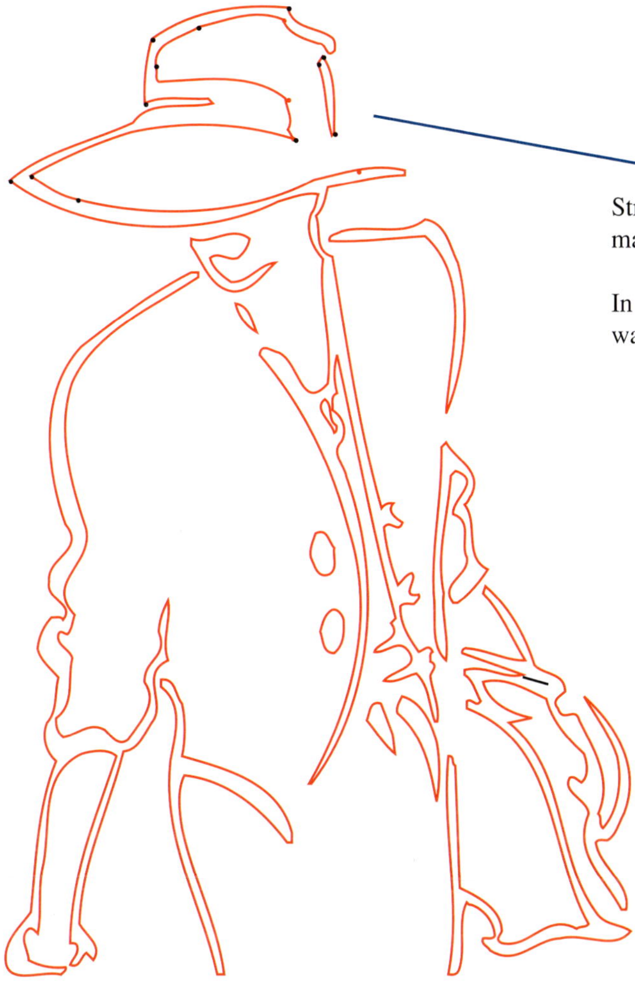

Streamline converts the image into line art which you may edit by moving, deleting, or adding points.

In this example, only the head of the illustrated woman was used, and the logo below was the result.

Adobe Streamline is a product of Adobe Systems Incorporated, 1585 Charleston Road, PO Box 7900, Mountain View, CA 94039-7900.

# Letraset Envelopes

Letraset Envelopes is an extension of Macromedia FreeHand and Adobe Illustrator. The product lets designers shape and distort individual letters, words, lines of type, and graphics with a click and drag of the mouse. In addition, users can add ripples, waves, and perspective to text and graphics by modifying any of the 200+ "envelopes" in this system.

The illustrations below show the basic element (top right), along with a sample of how that element would be modified in various envelopes. At right are a number of type modifications which were done using the envelopes.

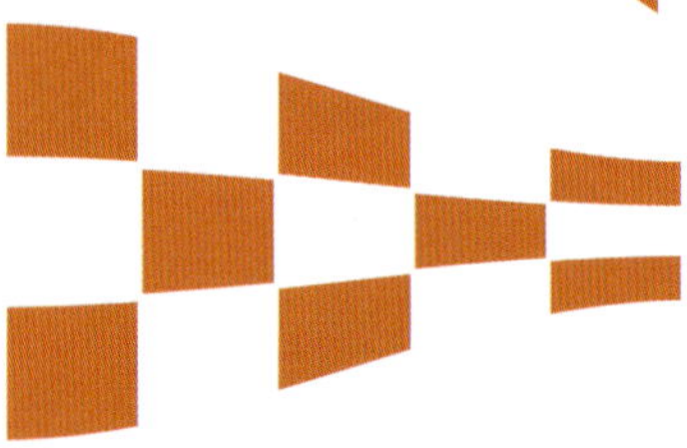

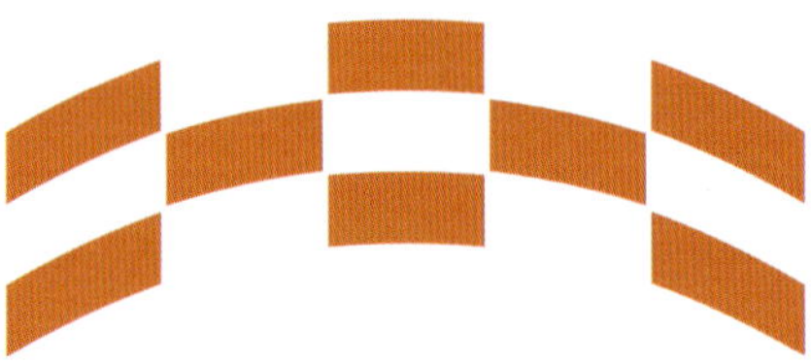

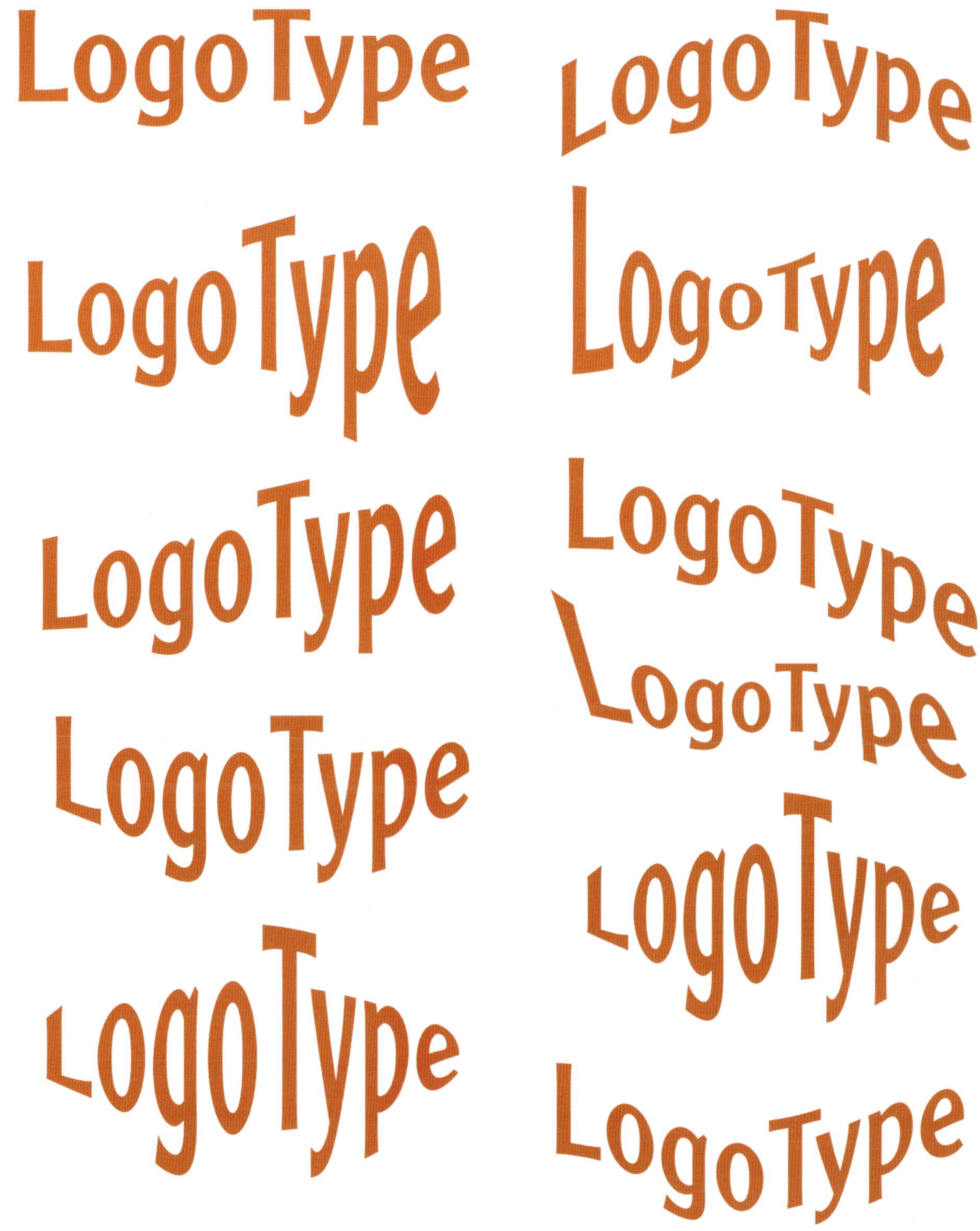


Letraset Envelopes is available from Letraset USA, 40 Eisenhower Drive, Paramus, NJ 07653. Phone: (800) 343-TYPE

# Adobe Gallery Effects 1.5

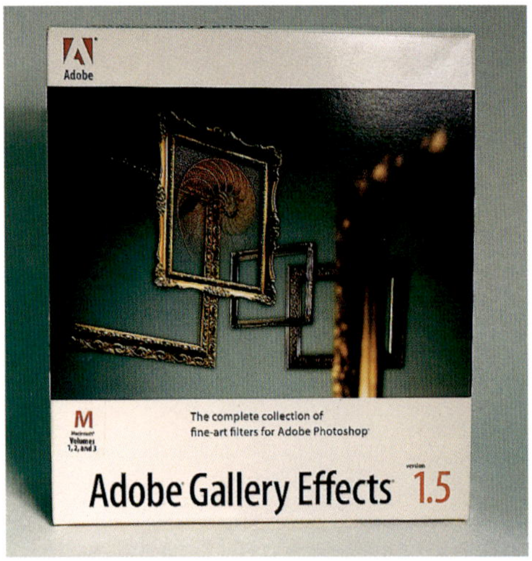


This three-volume set of fine-art filters is available for Macintosh and Windows. It can be used with various programs, but was specifically designed as Adobe Photoshop plug-ins. A total of 38 filters with a near countless number of adjustment options can make your stock photograph a true original.

A very nice (but surely unplanned) bonus with this product is that a low-resolution image will often produce the perfect image while using less memory than its high-res counterpart.

Original Image

Bas Relief

Chrome

Craquelure

Film Grain

Glass

Diffuse Glow

Graphic Pen

Mosaic

Notepaper

Patchwork

Plastic Wrap

Ripple

Rough Pastels

Spatter

Sponge

Reticulation

Stained Glass

Texturizer

Water Paper

Photocopy

Letraset Envelopes is available fromLetraset USA, 40 Eisenhower Drive, Paramus, NJ 07653
Phone: (800) 343-TYPE

# Xaos Tools Typecaster

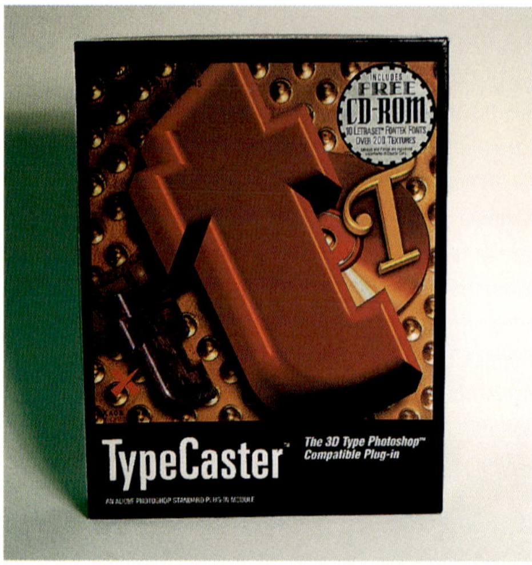


Typecaster is a three-dimensional type plug-in that is compatible with a variety of programs such as Adobe Photoshop, Adobe Premiere, Adobe After Effects, Fractal Design Painter, Macromedia FreeHand, Macromedia Director, Ray Dream Designer, Specular Collage, and others. The application lets you create 3D text with control over such parameters as lighting, textures, and bump maps. The companion CD also includes a large library of textures, bump maps fonts, and other graphic utilities you can use to further enhance your work.

Typecaster is available fromXaos Tools, Inc., 600 Townsend St., Suite 270 East, San Francisco, CA 94103. Phone: (415) 487-7000. Fax: (415) 558-9886.

# Auto F/X

Auto F/X is a large number of filters which can be used in Photoshop to modify any typeface, artwork, or scanned graphic (except photos). Modules available include Typographic Edges, Auto/Glow, Auto/Shadow, Auto/Path, Auto/Saturate, Auto/Screen, Auto/Textures, Auto/Emboss, and Auto/Focus.

The Auto/Textures filters alone include 1,000 different backgrounds, and all the modules are easy to use. You have multiple settings in each option, which give you a great deal of control over the finished graphic.

A basic star was used as the starting point for all these graphics. Each one is a different version of Typographic Edges.

3 versions of frogs using the auto-glow module.

These two globes, as well as two of the graphics below, use variations of the Typographic Edges feature. The ampersand (&) in the center uses the auto/shadow effect.

Auto F/X is available from Auto F/X, HCR 73, Box 689, Alton Bay, N H 03810. Phone: (603) 875-4400.

# Using Clip Art as a Logo

There will be two reactions to the above headline.

1. Some people will say: "You can use clip art for a logo  Neat." These people will be able to satisfy some clients in a cost-effective way.

2. Others will say: "I wouldn't be caught dead using clip art — at all."

Whatever your reaction, the final section of this book is for you. (Much like cartoons featuring a squirrel and an elk, or whatever, "clip art" has two levels of appreciation.

For the person who'd never, ever use clip art, the following pages show ... ah ... clip art that is really good. And if you'd never use it, you can still check out the neat graphic styles included in the next 40 or so pages. There are some very good illustration styles here which should trigger some ideas.

And—if you have the occasional need to use clip art for a logo project, the following pages show some really good sources. And, on each page, we produced a sample clip art logo to show the thought process which might involve stock art.

So, whatever your attitude about clip art, here's an excellent collection of graphics.

# Adopting Public Domain Clip Art as a Trademark

Although it might surprise, it is possible to adopt and use clip art to become one's trademark or service mark. The legal definition of a "mark" (whether a trademark or a service mark) is

> **Any Word, Name, Symbol or Device, or Any Combination Thereof Used to *Identify and Distinguish* a Person's Goods or Services from Other Goods and Services, and Used to *Indicate the Source* of the Goods or Services.**

Legally, clip art would be termed a "device" (as would any logo design). Consequently, it is possible to adopt clip art and use it as one's mark. However, note that the legal definition requires a mark to **identify and distinguish** the user's goods or services, and also to **indicate the source** of the goods or services. Because clip art by its very nature is public domain, as an initial matter clip art will difficult (but not impossible) to qualify as a mark, especially if clip art is used by itself as the mark. For example, there are many "little Italian men" in the clip art realm, and it could be problematic if one were to adopt one of the "little Italian men" as a mark for a pizza restaurant or a line of Italian sauces. The "little Italian man" clip art would be so common, it initially would legally fail to "distinguish" one pizza restaurant from another. In addition, it is quite possible that someone else would choose the same "little Italian man" logo for that person's pizza restaurant. In this situation, neither would acquire any protectible rights.

Therefore, if you intend to adopt clip art as a logo, it is recommended that you **also** use a unique word in association with the clip art logo. The combination would likely be protectible as a mark. Here is a real-life example. A client wanted to develop a line of "logo clothing". The client identified a pleasing piece of clip art (a rising pheasant) he wanted to adopt. We searched that design (it is *especially necessary* to search clip art designs, since by their very nature they can be commonly used) and determined that no one else was using a pheasant (or similar appearing bird) in the clothing area. Then, after we explained the problems associated with using "descriptive" words as a mark, the client adopted the unique term DANKRIST (the first syllable of his grandchildren's names) as a made-up word to be used in association with the "rising pheasant" design. The combined logo was appealing, and developed for very low cost.

Legal information provided by James R. Higgins, Jr., attorney specializing in trademark law;
Middleton & Reutlinger, 2500 Brown & Williamson Tower, Louisville, Kentucky 40202-3410

# Photogear Backgrounds

The backgrounds here are photos of actual flat objects. There are a number of businesses which can effectively use a logo which has some visual indication of just what the firm does.

Marble 12

Granite

Canvas

Denim

Marble 3

Plywood

The brick wall at left is one of the elements in the Photogear package. To create the logo below, we started with the brick wall, which was imported into FreeHand. Still in FreeHand, we set the letter "M" in type, then converted the letter to paths. The brick wall was then "pasted inside" the letter.

Next, that image (below left) was imported into Photoshop. We used the "Fire" filter from the Eye Candy software to create the burning wall logo shown below.

**Maiway**
**Fire Prevention**

Photogear Backgrounds are available from Image Club Graphics, 10545 West Donges Court, Milwaukee, WI. 53224-9967. Orders: (800) 661-9410. Catalog requests: (800) 387-9193. Fax: (403) 261-7013. Internet: www.imageclub.com

# Mountain High Maps; Globe Shots; Cool Maps; Earth Shots

This is a great collection of various globe shots, earth shots, relief maps, and other geographic representations that are excellent for use by a variety of companies. So you aren't global? Use a segment which shows your state or region. You can get a distinctive effect by taking any of these images into Photoshop and changing it, as we did with the globe to create the "Focus on Mexico" logo.

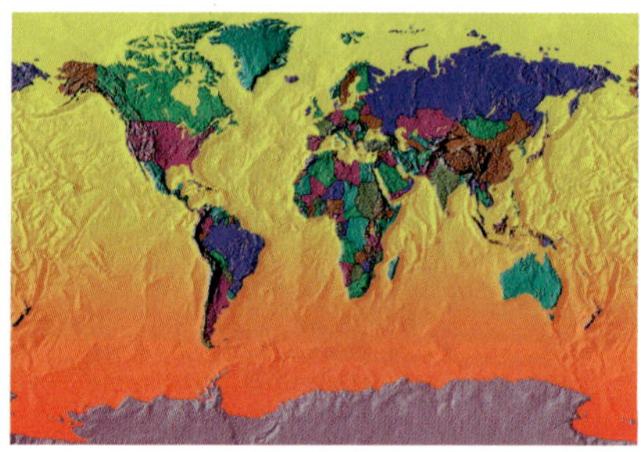

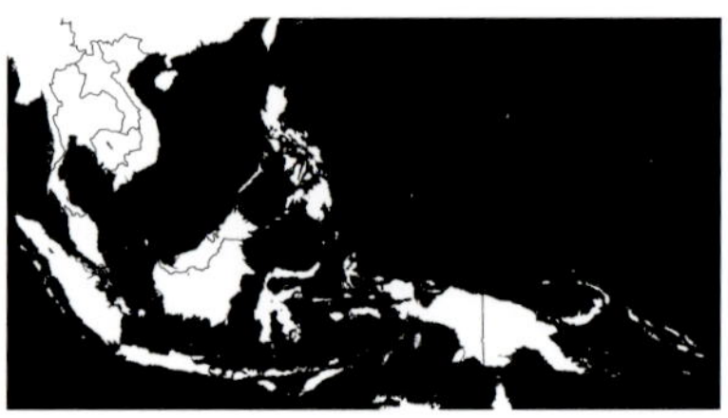

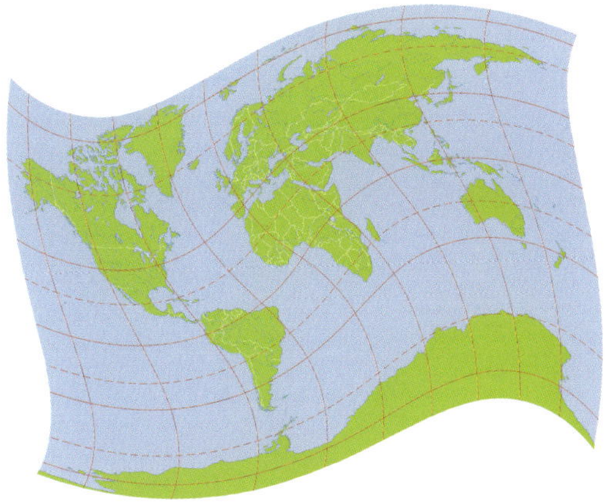

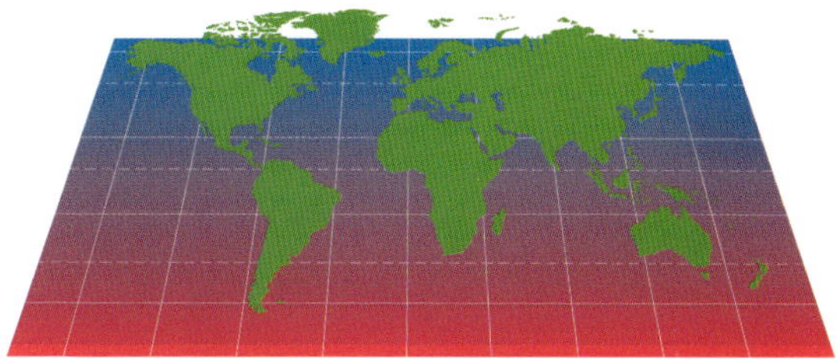

Mountain High Maps are available from Digital Wisdom, Inc. P.O. Box 2070, Tappahannock, VA. 22560.
Orders: (800) 800-8560.

# Letraset Phototone Alphabets

This collection is unusual in that it is composed mostly of photos of individual letters which were photographed from signs. In addition, there are a few complete alphabets (such as the typewriter keys). The inspiration here for design possibilities is almost limitless. For the project where using a single letter "Initial" logo is appropriate, this is a great starting point.

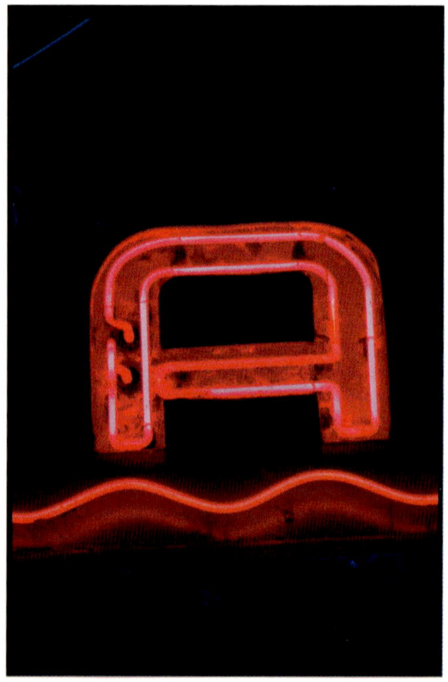

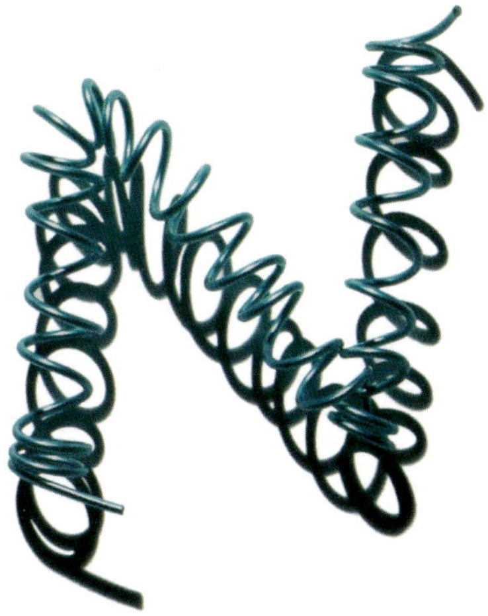

The many items in this software package present some interesting possibilities for creating an initial logo. To get the design below, we started with the element shown at left, then took it into Photoshop. We added noise, then used the color halftone filter.

A couple of minutes later, the finished image was complete.

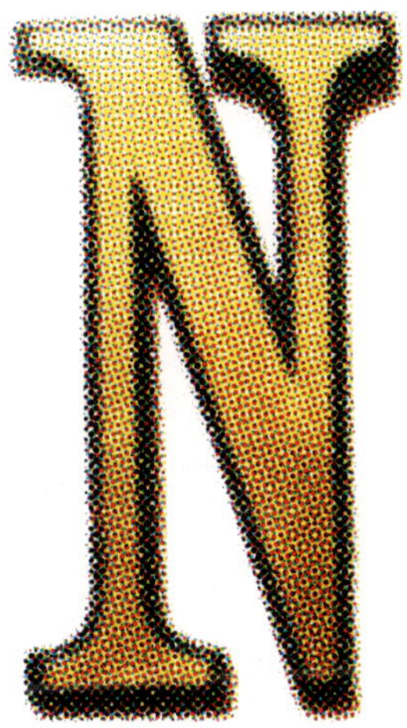


PhototoneAlphabets are available from Letraset USA, 40 Eisenhower Drive, Paramus, NJ 07653.
Phone: (800) 343-TYPE

# Digital Stock

Digital Stock has a great array of royalty-free stock photos. Categories include business, industry, fire & ice, space, animals, medicine, skylines, sports, leisure, tranquility, and much more.

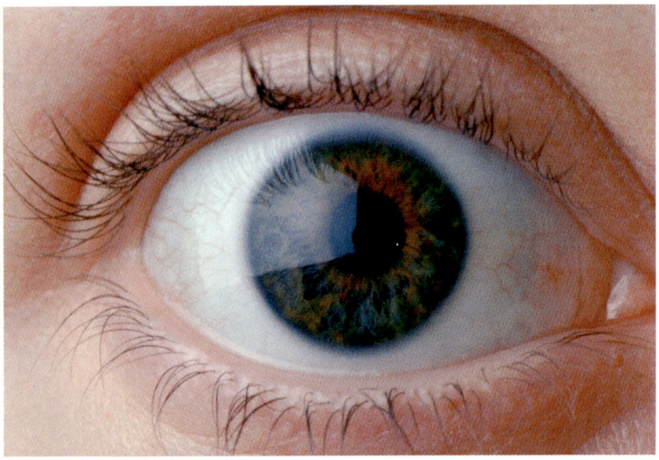

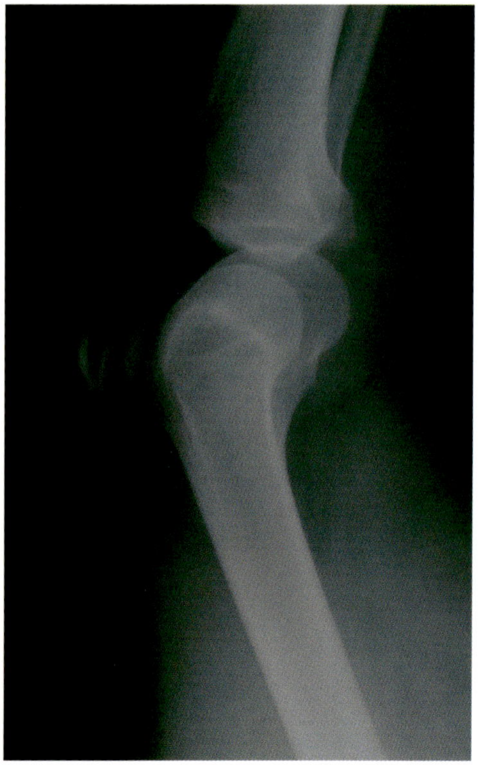

The right photograph can convey a very powerful and memorable corporate identity for a small business. There is a lot of royalty-free stock art available. Check it out.

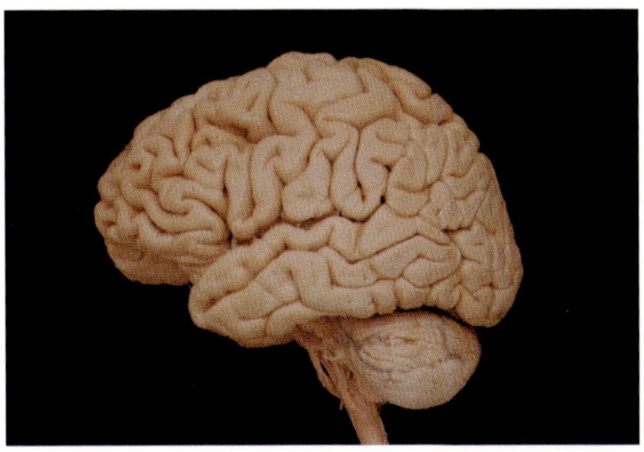

*Smart & Bright, Inc.*

Digital Stock products are available from Digital Stock, 4000 S. Sierra Avenue, Suite 100, Solona Beach, CA 92075. Phone: (800) 545-4514.

# Aridi Computer Graphics

Aridi has a number of unusual collections of art which can really dress up a company's identity. The packages include: Initial Caps, which has six complete sets of decorative letters in both color and black & white; Olde World Ornaments, featuring Celtic Arabesque, Victorian, Oriental, Russian and Art Nouveau designs; Ribbons, Banners & Frames; and Calligraphia.

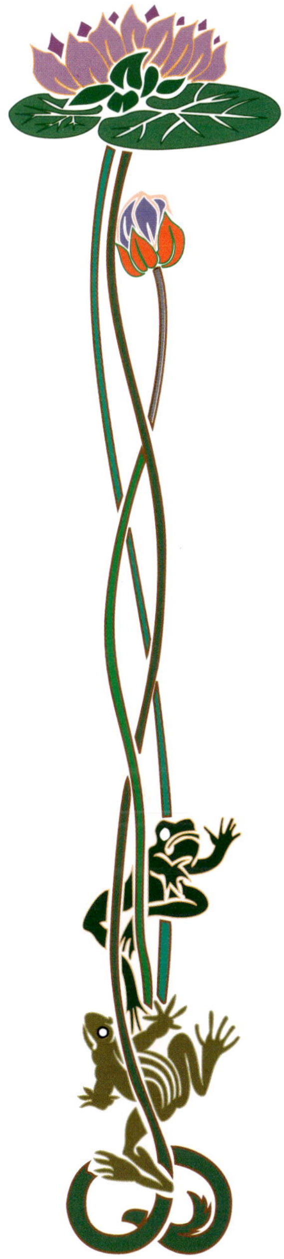

Aridi products are available from Aridi Computer Graphics, 5151 Beltline Road, Suite 815, Dallas, TX 75240. Phone: (214) 404-9171. Fax: (214) 404-9172.

# Classic PIO

This company specializes in royalty-free nostalgic theme clip photographs. Their library currently includes eight CD-ROM collections: Classic PIO Sampler, Classic Radio, Classic Telephones, Classic Microphones, Classic Nostalgic Memorabilia, Classic Business Equipment, Classic Entertainment, and Classic Fabrics.

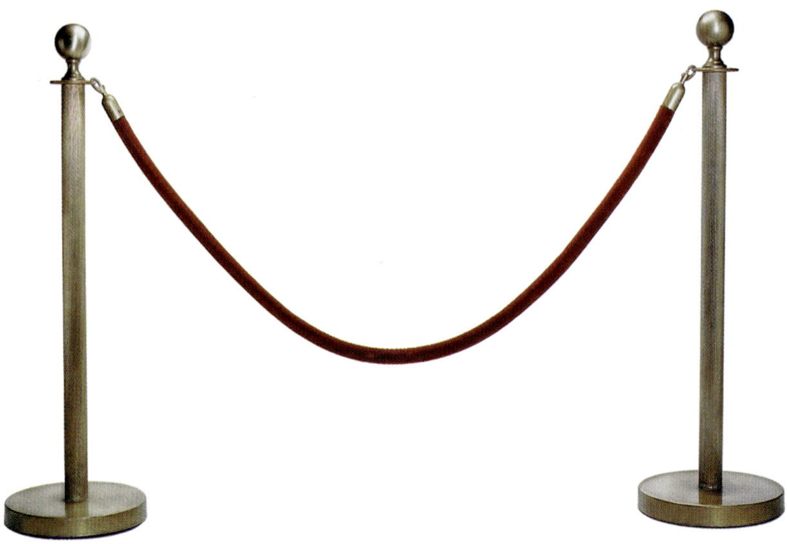

***James Wilson***

***Master Photographer***

*• 1160 Cyrus Way •*
*• Flatwoods, CA 94900 •*
*(415) 555-1111*

Many small businesses can create a highly professional look simply by using a distinctive photograph consistently on items such as letterheads, envelopes, business cards, invoices, etc.

Classic PIO Photos are available from Classic PIO Partners, 878 East Green, Suite 309, Pasadena, CA 91105. Orders: (800) 370-2746. Offices: (818) 564-8106. Fax: (818) 564-8554.

# Visual Language: Maps

Visual Language has a CD-Series with a vast array of antique maps, celestial maps, and really unusual items which can be used for businesses such as travel agencies, importers, etc.

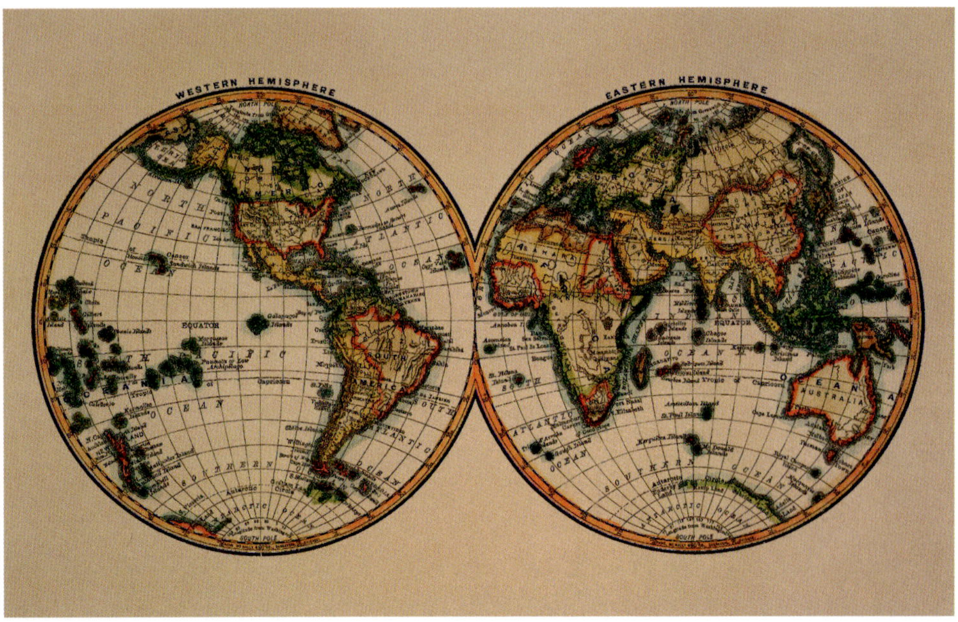

Marco Polo, Inc.

*Importing neat stuff from Asia since 1995*

Antique maps and related products are available from Visual Language, 569 S. Marengo Avenue, Pasadena, CA 91101. Product information: (818) 431-2777.

# Ultimate Symbol Design Elements

This is a collection of more than 3,000 visual elements, which can be used as stand-alone designs, or as the foundation for a more complex design. Categories include Sun, Moons, Stars, Flourishes, Typographic Devices, Pictorial Symbols, Dingbat Designs, Arrow Pointers, and Circular Designs.

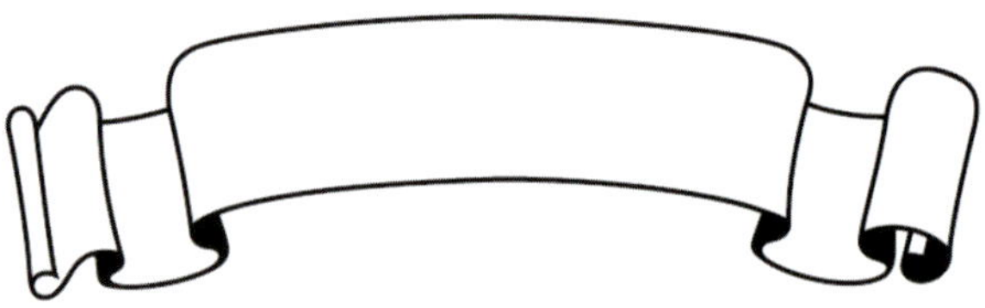

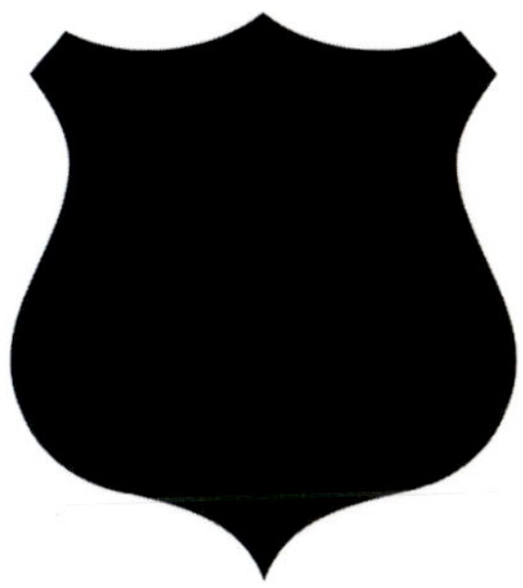

Design Elements is available from Ultimate Symbol, Inc., 31 Wilderness Drive, Stony Point, NY 10980-3447. Phone: (914) 942-0003; Fax: (914) 942-0004.

# CSA Archive Diskette Collection

An award-winning collection of black & white icons and illustrations from CSA Archive. Diskettes are available in Macintosh format only. Each of the Icon diskettes is formatted as a postscript Type 1 font so that every keystroke gives you a new image. The two illustration diskettes have been formatted in EPS.

# Russell Railroad

The CSA Archive Collection is available from CSA Archive, P.O. Box 581639, Minneapolis, MN 55458.
Phone: (612) 339-1263.

# CapTiles

CapTiles is a collection of more than 2,300 decorative letters, numbers, and symbols in 54 different style sets. Each is available in the following formats: *Macintosh*: EPS and PICT; *Windows*: EPS and WMF. The letters may be used quickly and easily to dress up low-budget corporate identity.

***A-One Desktop Publishing***

CapTiles is available from 3G Services, Inc. 23632 Hwy 99, Suite F407, Edmonds, WA 98026.
Phone: (206) 774-3518. Fax: (206) 771-8975.

# Transportation

Here is a large collection of crisp, clean transportation images. This package contains nearly every vehicle on the road, in the sky or water. In addition, there are strong visuals which apply to specific aspects of transportation.

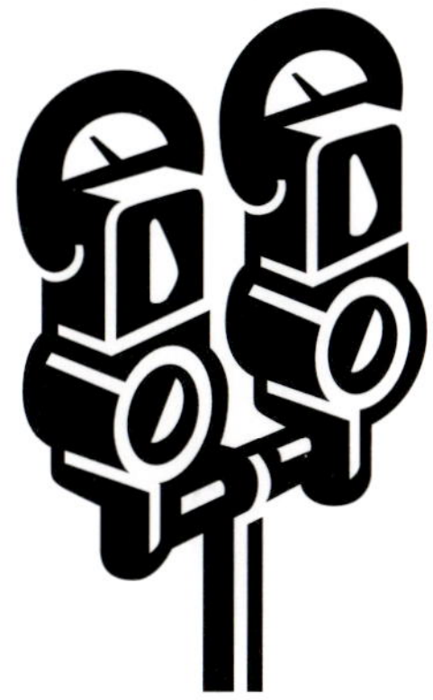

Transportation is available from Image Club Graphics, 10545 West Donges Court, Milwaukee, WI. 53224-9967.
Orders: (800) 661-9410. Catalog requests: (800) 387-9193. Fax: (403) 261-7013. Internet: www.imageclub.com

# Musicville

This collection from Image Club has black & white as well as color artwork in EPS format. Illustrator Guy Parsons has created a classy grouping of music images that are in categories such as ballroom dance, classical & composition, country, digital, the music business, and rock & roll.

Musicville is available from Image Club Graphics, 10545 West Donges Court, Milwaukee, WI. 53224-9967. Orders: (800) 661-9410. Catalog requests: (800) 387-9193. Fax: (403) 261-7013. Internet: www.imageclub.com

# Usefuls

This collection has an appropriate name as the pieces are all useful items found around the house. Need an image from the kitchen, medicine cabinet, garden shed, workshop, or office? You'll probably find it in this set of art from illustrator Carlos Aponté.

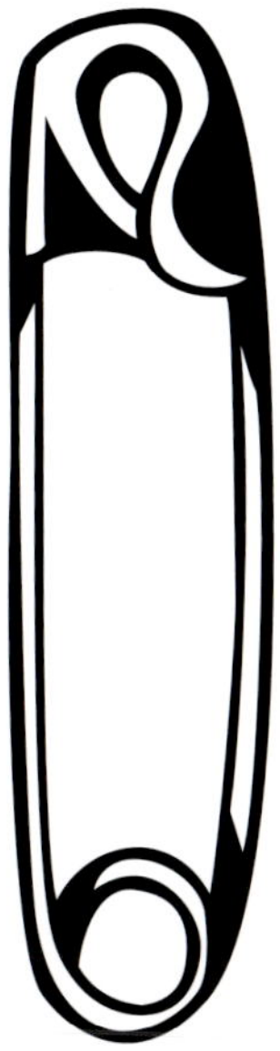

## Style

This stylish collection of illustrations drawn by New York fashion designer Carlos Aponté is filled with everything from the little black dress to exotic couture creations.

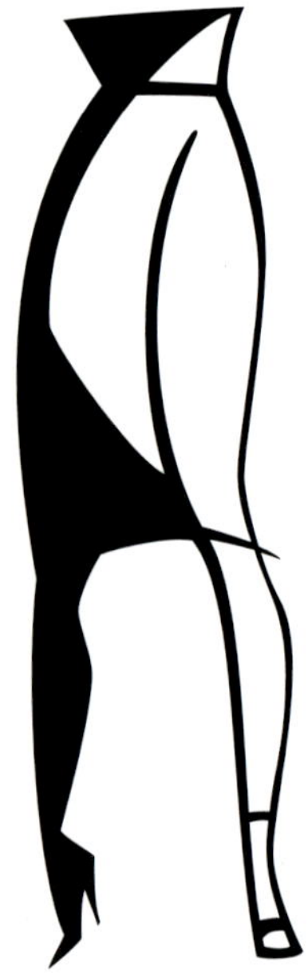

Style is available from Image Club Graphics, 10545 West Donges Court, Milwaukee, WI. 53224-9967. Orders: (800) 661-9410. Catalog requests: (800) 387-9193. Fax: (403) 261-7013. Internet: www.imageclub.com

# Neo Techno

This collection of images from the past, present, and future is done in a style that's decidedly space age. Designer Dana MacKenzie applied his technological look to a variety of different objects from different eras. All the images are in full color.

***Deenie's Weenies***

*Free Heartburn with Every Hot Dog*

Neo Techno is available from Image Club Graphics, 10545 West Donges Court, Milwaukee, WI. 53224-9967. Orders: (800) 661-9410. Catalog requests: (800) 387-9193. Fax: (403) 261-7013. Internet: www.imageclub.com

# Primal

Illustrator Jean McAllister has created a look of primitive cut paper images that's both timeless and universal. There is a variety of activities, objects, and events that provides a highly creative and unusual look. Images come in both color and black & white.

Primal is available from Image Club Graphics, 10545 West Donges Court, Milwaukee, WI. 53224-9967. Orders: (800) 661-9410. Catalog requests: (800) 387-9193. Fax: (403) 261-7013. Internet: www.imageclub.com

## Schoolsville

You'll find images from grade school to graduation in this unusual set of images. The unique style of designer Guy Parsons provides a highly memorable look. The images are in both color and black & white.

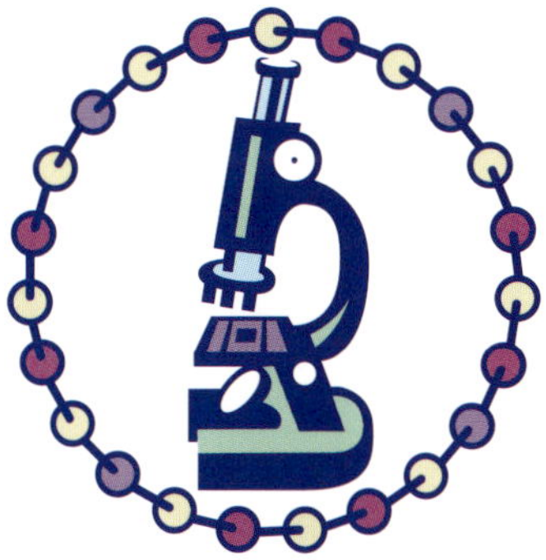

**My Dog Ate**
**My Homework**
***A Tutoring Service***

Schoolsville is available from Image Club Graphics, 10545 West Donges Court, Milwaukee, WI. 53224-9967. Orders: (800) 661-9410. Catalog requests: (800) 387-9193. Fax: (403) 261-7013. Internet: www.imageclub.com

# Woodcuts - Our Environment

This collection of 200 images takes you back to the fifties, when high-powered cars, jet planes, and rocket ships were fascinating novelties.

Woodcuts - Our Environment is available from Image Club Graphics, 10545 West Donges Court, Milwaukee, WI. Orders: (800) 661-9410. Catalog requests: (800) 387-9193. Fax: (403) 261-7013. Internet: www.imageclub.com

# Sketches Around the World

You'll find more than 200 EPS images in this collection, which includes activities, arrivals & departures, panoramas, destinations, and people of the world.

Many small businesses simply can't afford a custom logo design. High quality clip art can fill their budget needs, yet provide a quality image. This business card simply used one of the art images and a clean layout.

Sketches Around the World is available from Image Club Graphics, 10545 West Donges Court, Milwaukee, WI 53224-9967. Orders: (800) 661-9410. Catalog requests: (800) 387-9193. Fax: (403) 261-7013. Internet: www.imageclub.com

## Universal Symbols

There are more than 630 images in this neat collection, including animals, arrows, astrological symbols, geology, hands, international directional signs, mechanical, meteorology, photography, sports & recreation, shapes, and traffic control.

Combine good clip art with a little imagination, and you can come up with some good logos, such as these.

Universal Symbols is available from Image Club Graphics, 10545 West Donges Court, Milwaukee, WI 53224-9967. Orders: (800) 661-9410. Catalog requests: (800) 387-9193. Fax: (403) 261-7013. Internet: www.imageclub.com

# Strokes & Sketches

Simple, but fluid artwork offers a clean and free effect. This collection consists of nearly 250 images plus 40 color "swatches" for backgrounds that complement the art's style.

This elegant logo was done by using the leaping lady from the clip art, and simply adding a color bar to give dimension to the design.

I began this one with the teddy bear from the clip art collection (shown below). Then, I simply added a little color to give it life.

Strokes & Sketches is available from Image Club Graphics, 10545 West Donges Court, Milwaukee, WI 53224-9967. Orders: (800) 661-9410. Catalog requests: (800) 387-9193. Fax: (403) 261-7013. Internet: www.imageclub.com

# Woodcuts

You'll find 185 useful graphics in this collection, including animals, business & industry, food & drink, media, music, miscellaneous, sports & recreation, and tiles.

Start with a woodcut cactus. Add color, plus a catchy name, and you have a great identity for a business.

Woodcuts is available from Image Club Graphics, 10545 West Donges Court, Milwaukee, WI 53224-9967. Orders: (800) 661-9410. Catalog requests: (800) 387-9193. Fax: (403) 261-7013. Internet: www.imageclub.com

# Businessville

Guy Parsons has created a wonderful collection of modern corporate icons. Built on both traditional and cliched business imagery, this collection will never leave the impression that you are "Stuffy Big Business".

Businessville is available from Image Club Graphics, 10545 West Donges Court, Milwaukee, WI 53224-9967. Orders: (800) 661-9410. Catalog requests: (800) 387-9193. Fax: (403) 261-7013. Internet: www.imageclub.com

# Mini Pics

Mini Pics is a huge art collection—each volume has more than 100 images, and there are more than 35 different titles available. Each is actually in font format, so placing art is as simple as hitting a key. You use these in a program such as Illustrator or FreeHand, which allows you to convert the character into outline form. Then, you can modify the artwork any way you like. Three of the Mini Pic collections are shown here: ancients, confetti, and vehicles.

## Confetti

## Vehicles

## Ancients

The Aztec Club

Mini Pics are available from Image Club Graphics, 10545 West Donges Court, Milwaukee, WI. Orders: (800) 661-9410. Catalog requests: (800) 387-9193. Fax: (403) 261-7013. Internet: www.imageclub.com

# Nifty Fifties

This collection of 200 images takes you back to the fifties, when high-powered cars, jet planes, and rocket ships were fascinating novelties.

Nifty Fifties is available from Image Club Graphics, 10545 West Donges Court, Milwaukee, WI.
Orders: (800) 661-9410. Catalog requests: (800) 387-9193. Fax: (403) 261-7013. Internet: www.imageclub.com

# Neo Retro

This graphics collection is inspired by the fifties and is interpreted in a quirky modern style. Categories include heroes, home life, just folks, leisure time, technotronic, and working stiffs.

Neo Retro is available from Image Club Graphics, 10545 West Donges Court, Milwaukee, WI 53224-9967. Orders: (800) 661-9410. Catalog requests: (800) 387-9193. Fax: (403) 261-7013. Internet: www.imageclub.com

# Worldbeat Africa

The ancient and traditional African cultures are reflected in this collection which includes styles from Egypt to Zaire. You'll find a mixture of ceremonial masks, wildlife, ornamental medallions and borders as well as hieroglyphics.

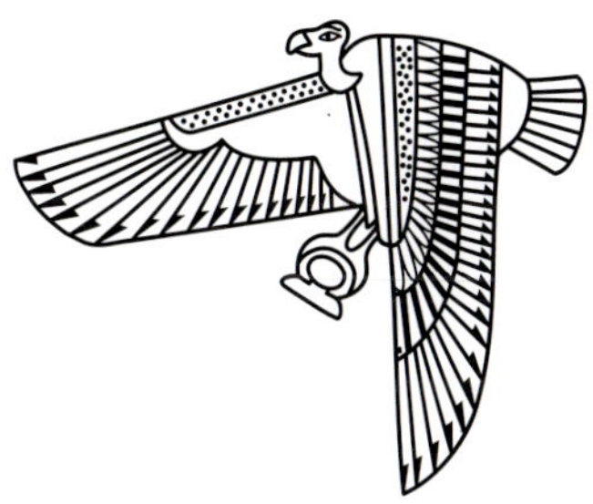

Worldbeat Africa is available from Image Club Graphics, 10545 West Donges Court, Milwaukee, WI 53224-9967. Orders: (800) 661-9410. Catalog requests: (800) 387-9193. Fax: (403) 261-7013. Internet: www.imageclub.com

# Art Jam

There's no easy way to describe this collection. You'll find banners, critters, edibles, going places, hardware store, home & office, kid stuff and making faces inn in a casual art style.

Art Jam is available from Image Club Graphics, 10545 West Donges Court, Milwaukee, WI 53224-9967. Orders: (800) 661-9410. Catalog requests: (800) 387-9193. Fax: (403) 261-7013. Internet: www.imageclub.com

# Pica Zoo

With Pica Zoo, illustrator Carlos Aponté goes back to the basics with elegant simplicity. Think of an animal that you need, and it's most likely in this unique collection.

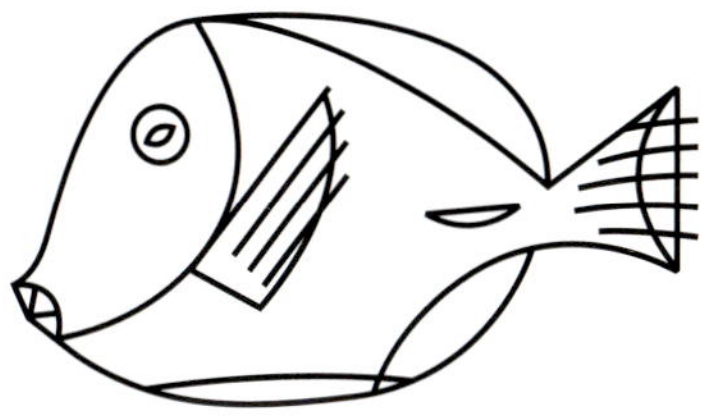

Pica Zoo is available from Image Club Graphics, 10545 West Donges Court, Milwaukee, WI. 53224-9967.
Orders: (800) 661-9410. Catalog requests: (800) 387-9193. Fax: (403) 261-7013. Internet: www.imageclub.com

# Index